The Splendor of Truth

The Splendor of Truth
A Critical Philosophy of Knowledge and Global Agency

BY
Januarius Asongu

FOREWORD BY
George Chrysostom Nchumbonga Lekelefac

WIPF & STOCK · Eugene, Oregon

THE SPLENDOR OF TRUTH
A Critical Philosophy of Knowledge and Global Agency

Copyright © 2026 Januarius Asongu. All rights reserved. Except for brief quotations in critical publications or reviews, no part of this book may be reproduced in any manner without prior written permission from the publisher. Write: Permissions, Wipf and Stock Publishers, 199 W. 8th Ave., Suite 3, Eugene, OR 97401.

Wipf & Stock
An Imprint of Wipf and Stock Publishers
199 W. 8th Ave., Suite 3
Eugene, OR 97401

www.wipfandstock.com

PAPERBACK ISBN: 979-8-3852-7047-7
HARDCOVER ISBN: 979-8-3852-7048-4
EBOOK ISBN: 979-8-3852-7049-1

VERSION NUMBER 01/19/26

Dedication

To Bishop Immanuel Balanjo Bushu, PhD, DD,
Emeritus Bishop of Buea, my Rector and Philosophy Professor at
St. Thomas Aquinas Major Seminary, Bambui—
whose wisdom and integrity first awakened
my vocation to think critically and believe intelligently.

To the memory of Professor Andrew Bongasu Tanla-Kishani,
my philosophical mentor and guide—
whose luminous mind and moral courage
made truth a lifelong pilgrimage of the soul.

To Professor Godfrey B. Tangwa,
whose scholarship and insight opened the door
through which I first encountered Karl Popper—
a discovery that transformed my intellectual destiny.

To the late Professor Bernard Nsokika Fonlon,
the Socrates of Cameroon—
whose synthesis of intellect and virtue
remains a beacon for African philosophy and public life.

To George Chrysostom Nchumbonga Lekelefac,
international advocate for the oppressed
and friend of the vulnerable—
whose fearless pursuit of justice embodies truth in action.

Together, these men shaped the philosophical and
moral architecture
upon which this work stands—grounding me in reason,
guiding me in faith,
and inspiring me to pursue the enduring splendor of truth,
the light that reconciles knowledge, justice, and love.

CONTENTS

FOREWORD | xxiii
PREFACE | xxvii
ACKNOWLEDGMENTS | xxxix

PART ONE: THE EPISTEMIC COMMAND—BUILDING THE CRITICAL TOOLKIT

CHAPTER ONE: THE BIRTH OF THE CRITICAL MIND—WHAT PHILOSOPHY REALLY IS | 3
    1.1 Introduction: Why Philosophy Still Matters | 3
    1.2 Philosophy as the World's Oldest Technology of Liberation | 4
    1.3 The Instruments of Liberation: The Three Tools of Philosophy | 5
        1.3.1 Critical Inquiry: The Courage to Doubt | 6
        1.3.2 Ontology: Mapping What Is Real | 7
        1.3.3 Epistemology: Defining the Rules of Knowledge | 8
    1.4 Philosophy as a Living Tradition: The Evolution of the Critical Mind | 8

CONTENTS

- 1.4.1 The Pre-Socratics and the Birth of Rational Inquiry | 8
- 1.4.2 Socrates, Plato, and the Ethical Turn | 9
- 1.4.3 Aristotle and the Codification of Logic | 9
- 1.4.4 The Islamic Golden Age and the Transmission of Reason | 10
- 1.5 Scholasticism: The Architecture of Reason | 10
- 1.6 The Enlightenment: Reason Becomes Revolutionary | 11
  - 1.6.1 The Rationalists: Certainty Through Thought | 12
  - 1.6.2 The Empiricists: Knowledge Through Experience | 12
  - 1.6.3 Kant's Critical Revolution: The Mind as Lawgiver | 13
- 1.7 Beyond Europe: Global Correctives to Rational Individualism | 14
  - 1.7.1 African Philosophy: Communal Personhood and Relational Knowing | 14
  - 1.7.2 Asian Traditions: The Wisdom of Balance and the Middle Way | 15
  - 1.7.3 Islamic Philosophy: The Bridge of Reason | 16
- 1.8 The Modern Fragmentation: From Positivism to Phenomenology | 16
  - 1.8.1 Positivism and the Cult of Science | 17
  - 1.8.2 Phenomenology: Reclaiming Experience | 17
  - 1.8.3 Analytic Philosophy: The Logic of Language | 18
- 1.9 Postmodernism and the Crisis of Truth | 18
  - 1.9.1 The Critique of Power | 19
  - 1.9.2 The Need for Reconstruction | 19
- 1.10 The Epistemological Turn: Knowing How We Know | 20

CONTENTS

1.11 The Twentieth Century: From Objectivity to Critical Realism | 21
    1.11.1 Scientific Realism and the Logic of Discovery | 21
    1.11.2 The Return of Value and Human Context | 21
1.12 The Digital Crisis: Epistemology in the Age of AI | 22
1.13 Toward Critical Synthetic Realism | 23
    1.13.1 The Need for a New Synthesis | 23
    1.13.2 The Four Pillars of CSR | 23
    1.13.3 CSR as Global Agency | 24
1.14 Philosophy as Moral Practice | 24
1.15 The Splendor of Truth Revisited | 25
1.16 Conclusion: The Responsibility of Reason | 26

CHAPTER TWO: THE PHILOSOPHY OF KNOWLEDGE—CRITICAL SYNTHETIC REALISM (CSR) | 27

2.1 Introduction: The Crisis of Truth and the Need for Realism | 27
2.2 Overview of the CSR Framework | 28
    2.2.1 The Dynamic Process of Critical Synthetic Realism | 29
2.3 Pillar I—Metaphysical Realism: The Ground of Objective Truth | 29
    2.3.1 The Adequation of Intellect and Reality | 29
    2.3.2 Truth and the Proposition | 30
    2.3.3 Rejection of Relativism and Perspectivism | 31
2.4 Pillar II—Epistemic Pluralism: The Dual Criteria of Warrant | 31
    2.4.1 The Correspondence Criterion: The Empirical Anchor | 31

CONTENTS

    2.4.2 The Coherence Criterion: The Rational Anchor | 32
    2.4.3 The Rejection of Consensus | 33
2.5 Pillar III—Critical Rationalism: The Dynamic Growth of Knowledge | 33
    2.5.1 Knowledge as Fallible Inquiry | 33
    2.5.2 The Logic of Falsification | 33
    2.5.3 The Scientific Method as Institutionalized Humility | 34
    2.5.4 Social Epistemology and the Chain of Warrant | 34
    2.5.5 Knowledge as Tentative Survival | 35
2.6 Pillar IV—The Axiological Distinction: Truth and the Integrity of the Intellect | 35
    2.6.1 Separating Validity from Value | 35
    2.6.2 The Ethics of Inquiry and the Intellectual Virtues | 36
    2.6.3 The Faith-Understanding Dynamic | 36
2.7 Pillar V—Epistemic Humility: The Tentative Nature of Knowledge and the Hope of Understanding | 37
    2.7.1 From Certainty to Responsibility | 37
    2.7.2 Knowing as Approach, Not Possession | 38
    2.7.3 Humility and Healing | 38
    2.7.4 Global Agency and the Ethics of Unknowing | 38
    2.7.5 Technology and the Humility of Reason | 39
    2.7.6 The Aesthetic Dimension of Humility | 39
    2.7.7 Toward a Human Ecology of Truth | 39
    2.7.8 The Splendor of Truth Revisited | 40
    2.7.9 Conclusion: Knowledge as Pilgrimage | 40

CONTENTS

CHAPTER THREE: KNOWLEDGE IN THE AGE OF ARTIFICIAL INTELLIGENCE | 41

   3.1 Introduction: The Age of Artificial Knowledge | 41

   3.2 The Machine as Epistemic Actor: Patterns Versus Knowledge | 43

      3.2.1 The Nature of Machine Learning | 43

      3.2.2 The Synthetic Structure of Knowledge | 44

      3.2.3 Optimization of Coherence: AI's Strength and Its Limit | 45

      3.2.4 Amplification of Testimony: AI's Power and Constraint | 45

      3.2.5 The Missing Sources: Reason and Experience | 46

      3.2.6 Synthetic Half-Knowledge and the Mirage of Understanding | 47

      3.2.7 The CSR Evaluation of AI Knowledge | 48

      3.2.8 The Human Role: Completing the Synthetic Loop | 48

   3.3 The Crisis of Digital Realism and Algorithmic Truth | 49

      3.3.1 The Epistemic Challenge of the Digital Age | 49

      3.3.2 The Prioritization of Engagement Over Correspondence | 50

      3.3.3 The Architecture of Isolation: Filter Bubbles and Echo Chambers | 51

      3.3.4 The Illusion of Omniscience | 51

      3.3.5 The Simulacrum of Experience: Deepfakes and Digital Fabrication | 52

      3.3.6 The Collapse of the Correspondence Criterion | 53

      3.3.7 The Algorithmic Manufacture of Reality | 53

      3.3.8 Algorithmic Bias and the Automation of Injustice | 54

3.3.9 The Human Cost of Epistemic Disorientation | 55
3.3.10 Toward a Renewed Digital Realism | 55
3.3.11 The Philosophical Stakes | 56
3.4 Criticality, Power, and the Ethics of Transparency | 57
   3.4.1 The Return of Critical Philosophy | 57
   3.4.2 The Methodological Crisis: Falsification and the Black Box | 58
   3.4.3 Transparency as an Epistemic Virtue | 59
   3.4.4 The Political Dimension: Knowledge and Power | 59
   4.4.5 Algorithmic Bias and Moral Realism | 60
   3.4.6 Situated Ethics: Context, Impact, and Responsibility | 61
   3.4.7 From Control to Care: The Ethics of the Critical Mind | 61
   3.4.8 Institutionalizing Criticality | 62
   3.4.9 The Ethical Horizon: Truth as Liberation | 63
3.5 Conclusion: Information Expansion and Wisdom Maintenance | 63
   3.5.1 The Paradox of Abundance | 63
   3.5.2 CSR as the Compass of the Digital Mind | 64
   3.5.3 The Moral Responsibility of Knowing | 65
   3.5.4 The Future of Reason: Coevolution, Not Competition | 66
   3.5.5 Wisdom as the Moral Apex of Knowledge | 67
   3.5.6 Restoring the Human Center | 67
   3.5.7 The Splendor of Truth in the Age of Algorithms | 68

CONTENTS

PART TWO: REFUTATION—CONQUERING THE FORCES OF IRRATIONALITY

CHAPTER FOUR: WITCHCRAFT AS PHILOSOPHICALLY UNJUSTIFIABLE | 73

4.1 Philosophy's Task of Refutation | 73
4.2 The Anatomy of Occult Causality | 74
4.3 The Historical Evolution of Witchcraft Thinking | 75
    4.3.1 Ancient and Medieval Roots | 75
    4.3.2 The Enlightenment and Skeptical Revolution | 75
4.4 The Failure of Epistemic Criteria | 76
    4.4.1 Correspondence and Empirical Adequation | 76
    4.4.2 Coherence without Correspondence | 76
    4.4.3 The Falsification Barrier | 76
4.5 Psychological Functions of Witchcraft Belief | 77
    4.5.1 Projection and the Shadow Self | 77
    4.5.2 Control and the Psychology of Fear | 78
    4.5.3 Cognitive Biases and Social Reinforcement | 78
4.6 The Sociology of Fear and Moral Order | 79
    4.6.1 Witchcraft as Social Explanation | 79
    4.6.2 Witchcraft Accusations and the Politics of Power | 79
4.7 The Theological Distortion of Faith | 80
    4.7.1 The Shift from Providence to Paranoia | 80
    4.7.2 Faith Seeking Understanding | 80
4.8 Liberation Theology and the Demythologization of Evil | 81
4.9 The Ethical Mandate of Truth | 81
    4.9.1 Intellectual Virtue and Moral Courage | 81
    4.9.2 The Duty of Deconstruction | 82
4.10 Refutation as Healing: The Therapeutic Function of Philosophy | 82
4.11 Conclusion: The Triumph of Reason | 82

CONTENTS

CHAPTER FIVE: EPISTEMIC FRACTURE AND THE CAUSE OF STAGNATION—THE CURE FOR UNDERDEVELOPMENT | 84

- 5.1 The Cradle, the Zenith, and the Paradox of Vulnerability | 85
  - 5.1.1 The Epistemic Ecology of Early African Civilization | 85
  - 5.1.2 The Age of Epistemic Leadership | 86
  - 5.1.3 The Paradox of Vulnerability | 86
- 5.2 The Epistemic Fracture—From Dynamism to Dogma | 87
  - 5.2.1 The Deification of Achievement | 87
  - 5.2.2 The Psychology of Dogma | 88
  - 5.2.3 Gerontocracy and the Death of Debate | 88
  - 5.2.4 The Four Failures of the Synthetic Loop | 89
- 5.3 Epistemic Underdevelopment—The Root of Material Poverty | 89
  - 5.3.1 Corruption as Epistemic Disease | 89
  - 5.3.2 The Epistemic Economy | 90
  - 5.3.3 The Paralysis of Occult Causality | 90
  - 5.3.4 Internal Fragmentation and the Logic of Weakness | 91
- 5.4 The Cure—Critical Thinking, Integrity, and Moral Renaissance | 91
  - 5.4.1 Reclaiming the Critical Mind | 91
  - 5.4.2 Reconstructing Education | 91
  - 5.4.3 Institutionalizing the Integrity Rule | 92
  - 5.4.4 Meritocracy and Epistemic Justice | 92
  - 5.4.5 Cultural Renaissance and the Media of Truth | 93
  - 5.4.6 A CSR Manifesto for Development | 93
- 5.5 Conclusion: Reclaiming Global Agency | 94

CONTENTS

CHAPTER SIX: REFUTATION OF DESTINY—THE FALLACY OF FATALISM | 95

  6.1 Introduction: The Universal Allure of Destiny | 95
  6.2 The Historical Logic of Fatalism | 97
    6.2.1 Ancient Roots: From the Fates to the Logos | 97
    6.2.2 Eastern Determinisms and the Search for Harmony | 98
    6.2.3 Theological Fatalism in Abrahamic Traditions | 98
    6.2.4 Modern Determinisms: From Mechanism to Algorithm | 99
    6.2.5 The Function of Fatalism: Psychological Refuge and Political Tool | 99
  6.3 The CSR Refutation of Destiny | 100
    6.3.1 Metaphysical Realism: The World Is Law-Governed but Open | 101
    6.3.2 Epistemic Pluralism: Correspondence and Coherence as the Tests of Truth | 102
    6.3.3 Critical Rationalism: The Demand for Falsifiability | 103
    6.3.4 Axiological Integrity: The Ethics of Truth and Freedom | 104
    6.3.5 Conditional Causation and the Logic of Freedom | 105
    6.3.6 The Epistemic Consequences of Destiny | 105
    6.3.7 Fatalism and the Death of the Future | 106
  6.4 The Psychology of Fatalism and the Myth of the Generational Curse | 107
    6.4.1 Fatalism as a Psychological Condition | 107
    6.4.2 The Generational Curse: Theologized Fatalism | 108
    6.4.3 Fatalism, Trauma, and the Need for Control | 110

CONTENTS

    6.4.4 The Cognitive Economy of Destiny | 110
    6.4.5 The Neuropsychology of Freedom | 111
    6.4.6 The Communal Dimension of Fatalism | 112
    6.4.7 The Liberation of Faith | 112
    6.4.8 The Counseling Perspective: From Determinism to Empowerment | 113
    6.4.9 The Global Variants of Fatalism | 114
    6.4.10 Summary: Fatalism as an Epistemic Addiction | 114
  6.5 Epistemic Sovereignty and the Ethics of Freedom | 115
    6.5.1 The Recovery of Epistemic Sovereignty | 115
    6.5.2 The Ethics of Freedom: Choice as Moral Obligation | 116
    6.5.3 Freedom and Contingency: The New Metaphysics of Hope | 117
    6.5.4 Education as the Architecture of Agency | 117
    6.5.5 Faith and Freedom Reconciled | 118
    6.5.6 Governance and the Integrity Rule | 119
    6.5.7 The Global Dimension: Freedom as Shared Epistemology | 119
    6.5.8 Freedom and the Splendor of Truth | 120
    6.5.9 Conclusion: From Destiny to Responsibility | 120

CHAPTER SEVEN: THE ETHICS OF EFFORT—RECONCILING CONDITIONAL CAUSALITY AND THE EFFICACY OF PRAYER | 122

  7.1 Introduction: The Philosophical Tension Between Agency and Petition | 123
  7.2 The Framework of Critical Synthetic Realism | 124
  7.3 Philosophical Justifications of Prayer | 125
    7.3.1 The Metaphysical Justification: Prayer as Divine Causation | 125

CONTENTS

- 7.3.2 The Psychological Justification: Prayer as Self-Transformation | 126
- 7.3.3 The Phenomenological Justification: Prayer as Encounter | 126
- 7.3.4 The Pragmatic Justification: Prayer as Moral Practice | 126
- 7.3.5 The Linguistic Justification: Prayer as Expression | 127
- 7.3.6 CSR's Synthesis: Prayer Transforms the Subject, Not the Structure | 127
- 7.4 The Answered Prayer Dilemma: The Crisis of Causality | 127
  - 7.4.1 Scenario A: The Mundane Answer (Epistemic Redundancy) | 128
  - 7.4.2 Scenario B: The Miraculous Answer (Epistemic Unwarrantability) | 128
- 7.5 The Ethical Hazard of Displaced Action | 128
  - 7.5.1 Abdication of Responsibility | 128
  - 7.5.2 Misallocation of Resources | 129
- 7.6 Work as Rational Devotion: The True Ethics of Effort | 129
- 7.7 Providence Without Partiality: The Ethics of Petition in a Conditional World | 130
  - 7.7.1 The Epistemic Contradiction | 130
  - 7.7.2 The Ethical Absurdity of Divine Favoritism | 130
  - 7.7.3 The Psychological Reality: Prayer as Performance | 130
  - 7.7.4 The Theological Reinterpretation: General Providence | 131
  - 7.7.5 CSR's Resolution: Providence Through Participation | 131
- 7.8 The Compassion of Realism and the Humility of Doubt | 131

CONTENTS

7.9 Epilogue: Faith, Effort, and the Silence of Heaven | 132

PART THREE: AGENCY—BUILDING THE RATIONAL SOCIETY AND THE GOOD LIFE

CHAPTER EIGHT: POLITICAL PHILOSOPHY—A DEFENSE OF DEMOCRACY | 137

    8.1 Introduction: The Political Architecture of Warranted Truth | 137

    8.2 Democracy as Institutionalized Falsifiability | 138

        8.2.1 The Political Synthetic Loop | 138

        8.2.2 Democracy as a Self-Correction Engine | 139

    8.3 The Social Contract and the Epistemic Covenant | 139

        8.3.1 Hobbes, Locke, and Rousseau Revisited | 140

        8.3.2 The Veil of Error: A New Construct | 140

    8.4 Doctrines of Democracy: Competing Models and Their Limits | 141

        8.4.1 Utilitarianism and the Tyranny of Numbers | 141

        8.4.2 Marxism and the Problem of Historical Certitude | 141

        8.4.3 Libertarianism and the Myth of Perfect Autonomy | 142

        8.4.4 Feminist and Communitarian Correctives | 142

    8.5 Diagnosing the American Experiment | 142

        8.5.1 The Senate: Arithmetic Injustice | 142

        8.5.2 The Electoral College and the Mirage of Majority | 143

        8.5.3 The Presidency: Reverence Without Accountability | 143

        8.5.4 Representation Without Representation | 143

        8.5.5 Money, Media, and the Collapse of Testimony | 144

CONTENTS

8.5.6 Lifetime Tenure and Judicial Rigidity | 144
8.6 Separation of Church and State: The Epistemic Boundary | 144
8.7 The Epistemic Republic: Democracy for the Age of Complexity | 145
    8.7.1 The Four Pillars of the Epistemic Republic | 145
    8.7.2 Digital Democracy and Algorithmic Accountability | 146
8.8 The Global Dimension: Planetary Democracy | 146
8.9 The Ethical Foundation: Truth, Responsibility, and Freedom | 146
8.10 Toward the Perfectible Democracy: The Best Theory So Far | 147
8.11 Conclusion: Liberal Democracy as Reason Made Social | 148
Interlude: The Epistemic Republic Manifesto | 148

CHAPTER NINE: THE ARCHITECTURE OF FLOURISHING—FAIRNESS, LOVE, AND THE ETHICS OF THE GOOD SOCIETY | 151

9.1 Introduction—The Teleology of Warranted Action | 151
9.2 Eudaimonia—The Harmony of Truth, Freedom, and Virtue | 152
9.3 Redefining Fairness—From Equality to Equity | 153
    9.3.1 Equality and Its Limits | 153
    9.3.2 Equity as Conditional Fairness | 153
9.4 Sustainability and Intergenerational Justice | 154
    9.4.1 Conditional Causality Across Time | 154
    9.4.2 Regenerative Design—Beyond Maintenance | 154
9.5 Love and Compassion—The Rational Heart of Ethics | 155

CONTENTS

9.5.1 Love as Epistemic Acceptance | 155
9.5.2 Warranted Grace | 155
9.6 Happiness—The Splendor of Alignment with Reality | 155
9.7 The Ethics of the Good Society | 156
    9.7.1 Epistemic Equity and Universal Education | 156
    9.7.2 Global Cooperation and Technological Ethics | 156
    9.7.3 Integrating Kindness—Beyond Legalism | 157
    9.7.4 Sustainability and Regenerative Civic Design | 157
9.8 Applied Ethics—Justice and Regeneration | 158
    9.8.1 Warranted Justice | 158
    9.8.2 The Regenerative City | 158
9.9 Toward the Eudaimonic Civilization | 158
9.10 Manifesto of the Flourishing World | 159

PART FOUR—ILLUMINATION: THE FULFILLMENT OF KNOWLEDGE

CHAPTER TEN: KNOWLEDGE AND TRANSCENDENCE—THE EPILOGUE OF TRUTH | 163

10.1 Introduction: The Horizon Beyond Knowledge | 163
10.2 The Limits of the Synthetic Loop | 164
    10.2.1 The Asymptote of Comprehension | 164
    10.2.2 The Metaphysical Horizon | 164
10.3 The Ethics of Mystery | 165
    10.3.1 Faith as Epistemic Humility | 165
    10.3.2 The Moral Dangers of Certitude | 165
10.4 The Convergence of Science, Art, and Spirituality | 166
    10.4.1 Science as Reverent Inquiry | 166

CONTENTS

    10.4.2 Art as the Bridge of Meaning | 166
    10.4.3 Spirituality as the Ethics of Connection | 166
  10.5 The Transcendent Function of Knowledge | 167
    10.5.1 Knowledge as Participation | 167
    10.5.2 The Evolution of Consciousness | 167
  10.6 Death, Meaning, and the Continuity of the Loop | 167
    10.6.1 Mortality as the Catalyst of Meaning | 167
    10.6.2 Immortality Through Contribution | 168
  10.7 The Future of Reason—Toward an Epistemic Republic of Humanity | 168
    10.7.1 Global Reason as Moral Imperative | 168
    10.7.2 Technology as the New Frontier of Moral Evolution | 169
  10.8 The Splendor of Truth—Final Reflections | 169
  10.9 Benediction: The Prayer of the Rational Heart | 170

EPILOGUE: Truth as Liberation—The Final Victory of Knowledge | 171

POSTSCRIPT: In the Light of the Unfinished | 175

APPENDIX I: The Conceptual Model of Critical Synthetic Realism (CSR) | 177

APPENDIX II: Glossary of Key Terms | 181

APPENDIX III: The CSR Method in Education and Policy—Practical Applications | 189

ABOUT THE AUTHOR | 193

BIBLIOGRAPHY | 199

INDEX | 205

FOREWORD
TRUTH AS LIBERATION—THE MORAL RADIANCE OF REASON

Philosophy, when at its highest vocation, is not a luxury of thought but an act of conscience. It is the discipline by which humanity measures its fidelity to truth, justice, and the moral order inscribed within creation. In this profound and ambitious work, *The Splendor of Truth: A Critical Philosophy of Knowledge and Global Agency*, Dr. Januarius Jingwa (JJ) Asongu restores philosophy to that original vocation. He reminds us that the love of wisdom must ultimately become the defense of human dignity, and that truth—understood not as dogma but as correspondence between intellect and reality—is the only foundation on which genuine freedom and justice can stand.

Dr. Asongu's contribution is both philosophical and prophetic. In an era dominated by noise, manipulation, and half-truths, he offers an intellectual architecture sturdy enough to rebuild the human spirit. His system, Critical Synthetic Realism (CSR), is at once a metaphysical foundation, an epistemological method, and an ethical mandate. It unites the rigor of reason with the humility of faith, demanding that every claim to knowledge, power, or morality be tested against the twin criteria of correspondence and coherence. The result is a unified vision of truth as both *splendor* and *discipline*—radiant because it liberates, demanding because it obliges.

As a canon lawyer and advocate for the oppressed, I approach this work from the standpoint of moral law. Law without truth collapses into tyranny; truth without law risks becoming abstraction. CSR provides the bridge between these domains. It calls for a world governed not by arbitrary decree but by warranted knowledge—knowledge that can withstand the scrutiny of evidence and reason. Dr. Asongu's Integrity Rule, that all public acts must correspond to verifiable reality, should be etched in the conscience of every judge, legislator, and educator. It is a philosophical articulation of what canon law and natural law have always affirmed: that justice is the application of truth to circumstance, and that the abuse of truth is the beginning of every form of corruption.

There is, in these pages, an unmistakable moral urgency. Dr. Asongu argues that the crises of our age—political, economic, and ecological—are not first material but epistemic. Humanity suffers, he insists, from a rupture in the relationship between belief and reality, between assertion and warrant. This Epistemic Fracture—the willful divorce of knowledge from truth—has made superstition, authoritarianism, and corruption inevitable. To repair it requires not merely new policies, but a new public philosophy: one that restores the correspondence between intellect, reality, and conscience. CSR is that philosophy. It proposes nothing less than an epistemic reformation—an age of reason reconciled with moral faith.

What is remarkable about Asongu's project is its breadth of synthesis. Drawing on Catholic moral theology, Aristotelian realism, Thomistic metaphysics, Popperian critical rationalism, and the African philosophical tradition of communal harmony, he fashions a system that is both universal and contextual. He insists that truth must be both local and global—tested by the lived experience of communities yet transcendent enough to unify humanity's diverse quests for meaning. In this, he stands firmly within the lineage

FOREWORD

of the late Professor Bernard Nsokika Fonlon, the "Socrates of Cameroon," and Professor Andrew Bongasu Tanla-Kishani, both of whom labored to reconcile faith and reason, revelation and reflection, Africa and the world.

For those of us who continue their mission—to defend the voiceless and uphold the sanctity of truth—this book is both a tool and a torch. It illuminates why ignorance is the first form of oppression, and why knowledge is the most enduring act of liberation. When Dr. Asongu writes that "truth is not static but dynamic—a living relationship between intellect and reality, tested through experience and sanctified by responsibility," he articulates a principle that resonates deeply with the Catholic intellectual tradition and with the heart of human rights advocacy.

The book's structure reflects a journey: from the epistemic foundations of knowledge, through the refutation of irrationality, to the construction of a rational moral and political order. Each part builds upon the last, culminating in a vision of Eudaimonia—human flourishing grounded in fairness, love, and happiness. In Asongu's moral universe, to know truly is to act justly, and to act justly is to love rightly. Love, for him, is not sentimentalism but the ethical manifestation of truth—the willingness to see and accept the other as they are, in their provisional and evolving humanity.

In our time, when democracy itself trembles under the weight of disinformation and cynicism, Asongu's defense of democracy as *reason made social* is a moral revelation. He shows that democratic institutions are not simply political conveniences but epistemic necessities. They are society's self-correcting mechanisms—its collective capacity for falsifiability, accountability, and moral growth. In the same way that science advances by testing and revising hypotheses, democracy advances by confronting and correcting its own errors. For Asongu, the vote is not just a civic right—it is an epistemic act, a participation in the great human experiment of truth-testing.

FOREWORD

But beyond its philosophical sophistication, *The Splendor of Truth* possesses a rare spiritual warmth. It is deeply Christian in tone, yet ecumenical in reach. It speaks to the priest and the philosopher, the scientist and the statesman. It invites each of us to rediscover faith—not as blind obedience but as moral courage in the pursuit of what is real. Reading this work, one senses that Asongu is not merely writing about truth; he is bearing witness to it.

I have long admired Dr. Asongu's intellectual and institutional achievements—from his founding of Saint Monica University and the American Institute of Technology to his advocacy for ethical education across Africa and the diaspora. Yet what this book reveals most clearly is the unity behind all those endeavors: the conviction that truth, when pursued with integrity, heals both the mind and the world. His is a philosophy that begins in contemplation but ends in action—an epistemology of hope.

For those who seek to reconcile faith and reason, or to rebuild the moral architecture of a fractured age, this book is indispensable. It stands as a testament to what Ambazonia, and indeed Africa, offers to global philosophy: a wisdom forged in suffering, disciplined by faith, and committed to justice.

In *The Splendor of Truth*, Dr. Asongu has given us not only a philosophy but a moral charter for the 21st century—a reminder that to live truthfully is to live freely, and that truth, in all its radiance, remains the surest path to liberation.

—George Chrysostom Nchumbonga Lekelefac

BPhil (Mexico); STB (Rome); JCL/MCL (Ottawa); Doctorandus (Münster)
Canon Lawyer, Human Rights Advocate, and Defender of the Oppressed
Written in Oklahoma City, Oklahoma, USA—2025

PREFACE
IN PRAISE OF THE LIGHT OF REASON

Truth has always shone more brightly than those who claimed to own it. From the first spark of human consciousness to the abstractions of modern science, the mind has been drawn irresistibly toward illumination—toward that which reveals, clarifies, and orders reality. Every age has named this longing differently: *Sophia* among the Greeks, *Veritas* among the Romans, *Aletheia* among philosophers, *Light* among mystics. Yet its essence remains constant—the intellect's yearning to behold what is.

BORROWING—AND RECLAIMING—A NAME

This book borrows its title from a text of immense theological influence: *Veritatis Splendor*, Pope John Paul II's 1993 encyclical on moral truth. My borrowing is deliberate but not derivative. Where the encyclical celebrated the radiance of revealed truth, this book seeks the radiance of discovered truth—the splendor that dawns when disciplined reason discloses the order of reality. Revelation descends; philosophy ascends. Both gestures honor the same light, but this ascent—the philosophical one—demands a different virtue: not faith's obedience but reason's humility.

PREFACE

The "splendor" in my title thus refers not to dogma but to illumination—the light that breaks forth when mind and world meet in honest correspondence. *The Splendor of Truth* is a defense of that light: an argument that truth is real, knowledge is possible, and reason remains humanity's most luminous faculty. It is a call to rescue truth from confusion, to restore reason as our moral compass, and to recover the dignity of knowledge as the foundation of freedom.

A World Darkened by Its Own Enlightenment

We inhabit a paradoxical age. Never before have human beings known so much, and yet never before has knowledge been so distrusted. Algorithms forecast our desires; data saturates our days; yet the very concept of objective truth is treated as antiquated. Post-truth politics, conspiracy culture, and digital tribalism have reduced truth to perspective. The relativist assures us that there are only interpretations. The cynic insists that truth is what power enforces. The sentimentalist declares that feeling trumps fact.

In classrooms and public life alike, I have witnessed the consequences of this epistemic confusion: anxiety, polarization, and the erosion of meaning. When truth becomes negotiable, the mind loses orientation; when every claim is "true for someone," nothing remains binding for anyone. Humanity begins to drift. What we face is not only a cultural or technological crisis but an epistemic one—a crisis of our very relationship with reality.

Philosophy, in its most vital form, must therefore regain its ancient courage. It must once again become militant in the defense of truth—not with weapons, but with clarity. The task of the philosopher today is not to invent new relativisms but to restore confidence in the possibility of knowing. This book is written in that spirit of intellectual resistance: a declaration that reason remains our most reliable path toward liberation.

PREFACE

FROM LIBERATION THEOLOGY TO THE PHILOSOPHY OF TRUTH

My intellectual journey began in the study of theology—not as a cleric, but as a seeker trained in the disciplined environment of a Catholic seminary. Those formative years immersed me in the great tradition of *fides quaerens intellectum*—faith seeking understanding. I encountered the passion of the prophets and the reasoning of Aquinas, the radical hope of Augustine, and the realism of Aristotle. Yet even in that environment of devotion, I sensed a question that faith alone could not settle: *What makes any claim true?*

The branch of theology that most captivated me was liberation theology. Its message was as simple as it was revolutionary: salvation without justice is blasphemy, and any theology divorced from human suffering betrays its own God. Liberation theology taught me that truth has moral weight—that a lie is not merely an intellectual error but a weapon of oppression. But I also saw that righteous passion, without epistemic rigor, easily becomes ideology.

To liberate the poor, one must first liberate thought. In the villages and classrooms of Africa, I saw how superstition and fatalism chained the human spirit as effectively as poverty itself. I realized that theology alone could not break those chains; it had to be joined by philosophy—by a method capable of distinguishing belief from knowledge, revelation from verification, inspiration from illusion. Liberation required epistemology.

Thus, even as I studied faith, I turned increasingly toward reason—not to oppose belief but to discipline it. The same God who commands justice also commands understanding. And the same oppressed mind that prays for deliverance must also learn to think critically about the causes of its suffering. From this conviction grew the first seeds of Critical Synthetic Realism (CSR)—a philosophy that weds the moral urgency of liberation theology with the intellectual precision of critical rationalism.

PREFACE

COUNSELING PSYCHOLOGY AND THE INNER LIFE OF TRUTH

If theology had shown me truth's social power, counseling psychology revealed its personal one. In my work as a counseling psychologist, I encountered truth not as abstraction but as healing. Clients came burdened by fear, guilt, or disorientation—often imprisoned by distorted perceptions of self and world. What liberated them was rarely persuasion or comfort; it was understanding. Insight, when achieved through honesty, had the power to restore agency.

I came to see that psychological healing is, at its core, an epistemic process. Distorted beliefs produce suffering; clearer understanding produces freedom. The therapeutic encounter mirrors the philosophical one: both demand courage to face reality as it is, not as we wish it to be. The mind, like the body, cannot heal on false premises.

From this practice emerged one of CSR's most fundamental principles—the Axiological Distinction: *truth must never be judged by how useful or comforting it feels.* In counseling, the temptation to soothe rather than enlighten is constant. Yet comfort bought at the expense of truth is merely anesthesia, not cure. The same principle applies to societies: nations too can live in denial, tranquilized by myths that spare them self-examination. My psychological training reinforced what theology had hinted at: truth is not always pleasant, but it is always liberating.

Thus, psychology gave CSR its human dimension. Where theology taught that truth emancipates societies, psychology taught that truth heals persons. The two converge in a single maxim: *to know truly is to live freely.*

THE BIRTH OF CRITICAL SYNTHETIC REALISM

CSR arose as a synthesis of these two worlds—the moral fire of liberation theology and the empirical discipline of psychology—forged together in the crucible of philosophy. It stands on four pillars:

1. Metaphysical Realism—affirming that truth exists objectively, independent of human belief.
2. Epistemic Pluralism—integrating Correspondence and Coherence as complementary criteria for warranted knowledge.
3. Critical Rationalism—acknowledging that human knowledge is tentative and must grow through falsification and self-correction.
4. Axiological Distinction—maintaining the integrity of truth against the seductions of utility, ideology, or comfort.

The resulting framework is both realist and humble, rigorous yet humane. It refuses to reduce truth to consensus or to enshrine skepticism as sophistication. It restores confidence in reason while preserving awareness of human fallibility.

Above all, CSR makes knowledge a moral act. To know falsely is not just to err but to betray the ethical responsibility of the intellect. To know truthfully, by contrast, is to participate in the world's own intelligibility—to share in the splendor of being. Through this ethical turn, CSR transforms epistemology into a philosophy of freedom: it teaches that every rational act is an act of emancipation.

REASON AND FAITH REVISITED

Because my early formation was theological, some assume CSR is a rejection of faith. It is not. It is a call to purify faith through reason—to distinguish what belongs to revelation from what belongs to verification. Faith, to remain healthy, must recognize the boundaries of knowledge; and knowledge, to remain humble, must acknowledge the mystery it cannot yet explain.

In this sense, CSR does not destroy faith; it refines it. It demands that faith respect evidence and that reason respect wonder. It invites believers to trust that truth and God, if both exist, cannot contradict one another. To test a claim is not to desecrate it but to honor the Creator by taking creation seriously.

Theology had taught me to love the light of revelation; psychology taught me to respect the shadow of the unconscious; philosophy taught me that both depend on the integrity of truth. The union of these three disciplines forms the heart of CSR—a system devoted to the radiant middle ground between certainty and chaos, between credulity and despair.

KNOWLEDGE AS LIBERATION: THE EDUCATIONAL MANDATE

Ideas must find flesh, or they perish as words. Philosophy, to remain alive, must descend from the page into the classroom, the community, and the public square. It was out of this conviction that I turned to education—not simply as a profession, but as a vocation of liberation.

The founding and leadership of Saint Monica University and its sister institutions—the IPS University Institute, the AHIT University Institute, and the American Institute of Technology—were guided by a single principle: education is not the accumulation of facts but the formation of reason. To educate is to emancipate. The school, at its best, is not a factory of credentials but a workshop of truth, where the human intellect learns to discern the real from the false and the just from the expedient.

From their inception, these institutions were designed to be laboratories of Critical Synthetic Realism in practice. Every program—from theology to technology, from business to psychology—was built on the belief that truth is not fragmented across disciplines. There is one reality, approached through different methods. The scientist seeks correspondence; the philosopher tests coherence; the ethicist measures consequence; the psychologist interprets meaning. All converge on the same horizon of intelligibility—the world as it is.

In a continent where education has too often been reduced to rote recitation and imported dogma, CSR sought to restore inquiry as the soul of learning. Students were to be trained not merely to repeat theories but to test them; not to inherit ideas but to interrogate them. A degree, I have always told my students, is not proof of wisdom—it is evidence of potential. True education begins when one learns to doubt responsibly.

EPISTEMIC POVERTY AND THE SHADOW OF SUPERSTITION

Africa's tragedy has never been a lack of intelligence but a lack of intellectual integrity—the historical inheritance of epistemic dependency. Colonial education taught the colonized what to think, not how to think. Postcolonial institutions often preserved the form of schools but not the freedom of inquiry. Superstition filled the vacuum left by critical thought. The village witch became the scapegoat for poverty; the political leader became the priest of destiny.

This epistemic poverty perpetuates material poverty. A society that attributes misfortune to invisible curses cannot design policy based on visible causes. The belief in occult agency becomes a moral anesthetic: it explains away failure and externalizes responsibility. To say "the spirits caused it" is easier than to ask "what did we do wrong?"

The task of philosophy, then, is not to mock these beliefs but to understand their psychological roots and replace them with epistemically warranted hope. CSR offers the conceptual framework for that transformation. It explains that the universe is causally closed—that every physical event has a physical cause—but that within this closure lies the open field of human creativity. We are not at the mercy of the unseen; we are the agents of the real.

EDUCATION AS THERAPY: THE SOCIAL ROLE OF THE PHILOSOPHER

My training in counseling psychology taught me that ignorance is not merely a deficit of information but a defense mechanism—a way of protecting the self from anxiety. Likewise, the persistence of superstition is not simply stupidity but collective trauma. Entire cultures that have suffered colonization, war, or exploitation often retreat into magical thinking as a coping strategy. The philosopher's role, then, is not to condemn but to counsel—to lead minds gently from illusion to insight.

In this sense, philosophy becomes therapy for civilization. Just as the therapist listens before interpreting, the philosopher must understand before correcting. One must discern why a people believe what they believe—what emotional, historical, or existential need that belief serves—before offering the alternative of reason. The transition from myth to science, from belief to knowledge, is not merely intellectual; it is psychological and moral.

That is why I often describe CSR as both a philosophy of truth and a therapy of knowledge. It treats falsehood not only as error but as illness—a distortion to be healed through understanding. Education, then, becomes collective counseling: a dialogue between fear and reason, between the inherited and the verified. The teacher's task is to mediate that dialogue with patience, empathy, and intellectual rigor.

TRUTH AS AN ETHICAL OBLIGATION

In both philosophy and psychology, I have learned that truth is not optional. It is an ethical commandment. The philosopher may discover it; the counselor must protect it. When truth is betrayed—whether by ideology or by ignorance—human dignity is the first casualty.

CSR asserts that truth has two dimensions: the objective (what is) and the moral (our obligation to align with it). Knowledge is not morally neutral because every falsehood tolerated sustains some form of injustice. Lies protect the powerful but also enslave the weak. To defend truth, then, is to engage in social justice.

This conviction transforms epistemology into ethics. It is not enough to know the truth; one must live by it. The student who cheats on an exam, the politician who falsifies data, the preacher who manipulates fear—all violate the same moral law: the correspondence between word and world. CSR demands the restoration of this integrity at every level of human interaction. It teaches that the smallest lie weakens the whole architecture of reason, just as the smallest infection threatens the body.

When truth becomes the measure of morality, freedom follows. A person who knows what is real cannot easily be deceived; a society that prizes accuracy cannot easily be enslaved. This is why the defense of truth is always the defense of freedom. The battle for the intellect is the battle for the human soul.

THE LIGHT THAT LIBERATES

The splendor of truth is not an aesthetic metaphor; it is a moral reality. Light, in every tradition, symbolizes revelation—not the mystical disclosure of secret doctrines, but the unveiling of what has always been present. When light enters, darkness does not fight; it disappears. The same is true of ignorance. To dispel it, one must not shout it down but illuminate it.

This book is, therefore, an act of illumination. It gathers insights from theology, philosophy, computer science, business, communication, linguistics, and psychology—disciplines that have each shaped my intellectual life—and fuses them into a single beam aimed at one enduring goal: to restore humanity's faith in reason and its capacity for truth.

In doing so, it proposes that knowledge is not merely *power*, as the modern world so often claims, but *peace*—the reconciliation of the human mind with the real. When reason and reality meet without distortion, the result is harmony: in the intellect, in the individual, and in society.

The pages that follow therefore invite the reader not into dogma but into dialogue—a lifelong practice of seeking, testing, and refining. Philosophy, properly understood, is not the art of having opinions but the discipline of eliminating error. Its final promise is not omniscience but serenity: the quiet confidence of a mind that dwells in truth.

To think is to see. To know is to be free. And to live in the splendor of truth is to live, finally, in the light.

THE STRUCTURE OF THE WORK

The book unfolds in three movements that mirror the life of the mind itself.

Part I, "The Epistemic Command," constructs the foundation—defining philosophy as the disciplined love of wisdom and developing CSR as a modern philosophy of knowledge. It equips the reader with the critical tools necessary to distinguish truth from belief.

Part II, "Refutation," applies these tools to humanity's oldest illusions—witchcraft, destiny, and the magical thinking that turns prayer into passivity. Here, CSR becomes a philosophical sword, cutting through the veils of unwarranted conjecture that enslave both individuals and societies.

Part III, "Agency," rebuilds what the second part dismantles. It shows how truth, once liberated from superstition, becomes the basis for ethics, democracy, and the good life. The final chapters

PREFACE

explore how fairness, love, and happiness emerge not from faith or fate but from understanding—from the conscious alignment of will and reason.

Together, these parts constitute a single moral argument: that the pursuit of truth is not an academic exercise but the foundation of human freedom. To know truly is to act freely; to act freely is to live justly.

—Januarius Asongu, PhD

    Townsend, Delaware, United States
    January 2026

ACKNOWLEDGMENTS

This work is dedicated first and foremost to those whose love, intellect, and presence have shaped my deepest convictions about truth and human flourishing.

To my son, Jude Jingwa Ngangsic-Asongu, whose insight and questions have compelled me to rethink many of my previously held assumptions. In his curiosity, I have witnessed Karl Popper's great insight come alive—that knowledge is never final but always progressive and self-correcting. Jude not only sharpened the ideas in this book but also assisted in editing the manuscript, offering thoughtful critiques with a maturity beyond his years. He has become both my most loyal critic and my most inspiring teacher.

To my daughter, Maria Yorkza Ngangsic-Asongu, whose empathy and quiet strength continually remind me that wisdom is sustained not only by reason, but by compassion. And to my son, Bernard Nkengbeza Ngangsic-Asongu, whose humor and boundless imagination keep philosophy from ever becoming too solemn. Together, they embody the living splendor of truth—curious, kind, and unafraid.

To my wife, Christine Ngangsic, my partner in every sense—intellectually, spiritually, and emotionally. Her love has been a steadying force, but so too has her extraordinary sacrifice. Christine

ACKNOWLEDGMENTS

supported our family financially while I took unpaid time away from work to write this book and others. I could not have undertaken a project of this magnitude while working full-time, and I could not have taken such time off without her unwavering commitment to our home. This book exists because she made space—through courage, generosity, and faith—for me to think, write, and create. She has taught me that love itself is a form of critical inquiry: the courage to see another person truthfully and to remain, through all provisional imperfections, committed to their becoming.

I am profoundly grateful to my parents, Dr. Nicholas Jingwa Asongu and Lady Monique Nkengbeza, whose example and sacrifices laid the foundation for everything I am. They instilled in me the enduring values of hard work, family, compassion for the underprivileged, love of education, and an unshakable faith in God. The philosophical and moral architecture of this book rests upon the virtues they quietly lived.

My intellectual journey owes an oversized debt to Karl Popper, whose philosophy has shaped Critical Synthetic Realism more deeply than any other thinker. Yet I may never have encountered Popper had it not been for Professor Godfrey B. Tangwa, the distinguished Cameroonian philosopher and Popper scholar. His early 1990s monograph on Popper was placed in my hands by Bishop Emmanuel B. Bushu, PhD, DD—then my rector and professor of philosophy at St. Thomas Aquinas Major Seminary, Bambui—who asked me to review the work. Until that moment, Popper had never appeared in our strictly scholastic curriculum. That unexpected encounter altered the trajectory of my intellectual life. Through Tangwa and Bishop Bushu, I discovered a philosophy of openness, fallibilism, and critical inquiry that has since become a foundational pillar of CSR.

To the late Professor Andrew Bongasu Tanla-Kishani, my philosophical mentor and guide, whose brilliance and integrity made philosophy a moral vocation rather than an academic exercise;

ACKNOWLEDGMENTS

and to the late Professor Bernard Nsokika Fonlon, the Socrates of Cameroon, whose synthesis of intellect, virtue, and civic duty continues to illuminate African thought. Their lives remain enduring arguments that truth and goodness are inseparable.

To George Nchumbonga Lekelefac, International Advocate for the Oppressed and Voice of the Voiceless—your fearless pursuit of justice across nations stands as a living embodiment of philosophy in action. You remind us that truth must never be divorced from courage. Thank you for being the first reviewer of this work and for graciously agreeing to write the Foreword.

I am equally indebted to my colleagues and students at Saint Monica University, the Institute of Professional Studies, and the American Institute of Technology, whose dialogue, critique, and dedication have continually refined my ideas. Each question, disagreement, and discovery has contributed to the Synthetic Loop of learning that gives this philosophy its living form.

Finally, I acknowledge the grace of God, the eternal Ground of Truth and Being. If anything in these pages carries light or coherence, it is because divine wisdom allowed my own provisional reason to participate, however humbly, in the infinite act of creation.

May this work honor all those—past, present, and future—who believe that knowledge, pursued with integrity and love, remains humanity's truest path to liberation.

PART ONE: THE EPISTEMIC COMMAND—BUILDING THE CRITICAL TOOLKIT

CHAPTER ONE: THE BIRTH OF THE CRITICAL MIND— WHAT PHILOSOPHY REALLY IS

1.1 INTRODUCTION: WHY PHILOSOPHY STILL MATTERS

Every civilization has produced its prophets, engineers, and revolutionaries—but only philosophy has produced a sustained method for asking *why*. In an age dominated by technology, speed, and distraction, philosophy might seem a relic of slower times—a luxury for academics rather than a necessity for societies. Yet the crises that define our century—climate collapse, digital misinformation, artificial intelligence, ethical disorientation—are not primarily technical. They are epistemological crises, failures of how we know.

Philosophy, far from being obsolete, is the only discipline equipped to address such crises at their roots. It teaches us not what to think, but how to think—how to test assumptions, weigh evidence, and recognize error. It is the intellectual immune system of civilization. Where politics, religion, or commerce pursue power, persuasion, and profit, philosophy seeks something far rarer: clarity.

PART ONE: THE EPISTEMIC COMMAND

If theology is the discipline of revelation and science the discipline of discovery, philosophy is the discipline of reflection—the capacity to examine the foundations of all other forms of knowledge. Its Greek name, *philosophia*, literally means "the love of wisdom," but this love is not passive admiration. It is an active discipline, a rigorous courtship with truth conducted through reason, dialogue, and the courage to doubt.

To philosophize is to resist captivity—to rebel against inherited illusions and lazy certainties. The first philosophers were not professors but dissidents. Socrates defied Athens; Descartes challenged dogma; Kant redefined reason itself. In every age, philosophy has functioned as the technology of liberation, freeing minds from superstition and societies from tyranny.

This chapter introduces that long struggle—the birth, maturation, and global evolution of the critical mind. It explains how philosophy, as both method and worldview, became the foundation of knowledge and the precondition for human agency. In tracing this evolution, we prepare the ground for the framework of *Critical Synthetic Realism (CSR)*, which will later emerge as philosophy's most recent synthesis: a defense of truth and an instrument for freedom.

1.2 PHILOSOPHY AS THE WORLD'S OLDEST TECHNOLOGY OF LIBERATION

Philosophy begins wherever human beings ask not merely *what* or *how*, but *why*. The earliest myths told stories to explain the sun, the sea, and death; philosophers replaced stories with arguments. Where myth attributed storms to divine anger, philosophy asked about atmospheric pressure. Where kings justified rule by ancestry, philosophy asked about justice.

This shift—from obedience to inquiry—is the origin of the critical mind. It is not merely intellectual but moral, for it demands

CHAPTER ONE: THE BIRTH OF THE CRITICAL MIND

courage: the willingness to live without absolute certainty. To think philosophically is to accept the risk of freedom.

Throughout history, human beings have faced two intertwined forms of bondage:

1. Physical bondage—the material constraints of tyranny, hunger, and disease.
2. Mental bondage—the invisible chains of superstition, prejudice, fatalism, and dogma.

Science and politics address the first; philosophy addresses the second. No reform or revolution can endure unless minds are first emancipated from illusion.

To grasp this point, consider two civilizations facing drought. In the first, people believe the gods have withdrawn rain as punishment. They perform sacrifices, waiting for divine mercy. In the second, they understand that rainfall obeys physical laws. They build irrigation systems and reservoirs. The difference between these two responses—the first supplication, the second agency—is the difference philosophy makes. It is the difference between *belief* and *knowledge*, between powerlessness and progress.

Falsehood always limits action because it distorts reality. To believe wrongly is to act ineffectively. Philosophy is humanity's most systematic tool for eliminating falsehood and discovering warranted knowledge—beliefs that correspond to reality and can therefore sustain agency. In this sense, philosophy is a moral enterprise. To think clearly is to act freely.

1.3 THE INSTRUMENTS OF LIBERATION: THE THREE TOOLS OF PHILOSOPHY

Philosophy as a practice of liberation operates through three interlocking instruments: critical inquiry, ontology, and epistemology.

Each represents a distinct mode of questioning that, together, form the anatomy of rational thought.

1.3.1 Critical Inquiry: The Courage to Doubt

Philosophy's first tool is *critical inquiry*—the disciplined act of questioning the unquestioned. This requires what the ancients called *parrhesia*—fearless speech—and what modern psychologists call cognitive openness. To engage in critical inquiry is to transform passive belief into active investigation.

The central questions of critical inquiry are deceptively simple:

- Why do I believe this?
- What is the evidence supporting this claim?
- What follows if it is false?

This is the moment when thought becomes autonomous. As René Descartes demonstrated through his methodic doubt, the refusal to take anything for granted—even one's own existence—was not a gesture of skepticism but of liberation.[1] By doubting everything, Descartes found one indubitable fact: *Cogito, ergo sum*—I think, therefore I am. From this insight, modern subjectivity was born: the idea that the human mind, not tradition or revelation, is the final arbiter of truth.

Critical inquiry, however, extends far beyond Cartesian introspection. It is also social and political. When Socrates asked his fellow Athenians to justify their moral beliefs, he was not merely playing logic games; he was engaging in moral surgery. His questioning exposed contradictions in the city's values, forcing his interlocutors to see that much of what they called "justice" was mere convention. The philosopher's method is therefore subversive: it replaces conformity with comprehension.

---

1. Descartes, *Meditations*.

CHAPTER ONE: THE BIRTH OF THE CRITICAL MIND

1.3.2 Ontology: Mapping What Is Real

The second tool is ontology—the study of being. Before we can know *how* to live, we must know *what* exists. Are we free agents or determined mechanisms? Is the universe material, spiritual, or dual? Are moral values objective or constructed?

Ontology provides the map of reality upon which all ethics and science depend. But this map has always been contested.

Early thinkers like Thales of Miletus (c. 600 BCE) proposed that all things arise from a single substance—water—an astonishing claim for its time because it replaced mythological multiplicity with rational unity. Heraclitus (c. 500 BCE) countered that reality was not substance but process: "Everything flows" (*panta rhei*). His notion of the *Logos*—the rational principle governing change—prefigured modern systems theory.

Ontology matured as philosophers realized that mapping reality required understanding causation, substance, and form. Aristotle's *Metaphysics* (c. 340 BCE) formalized these questions, distinguishing potentiality from actuality and asserting that every being has a purpose (*telos*). This teleological vision dominated Western thought for centuries, giving rise to both theology and early science.

Yet ontology also carries danger. When untested, it easily hardens into dogma. For millennia, metaphysical systems—Plato's Forms, Aquinas's Great Chain of Being—were treated as unquestionable realities. The eventual failure to achieve consensus among metaphysicians exposed a crucial insight: before we can map the world, we must calibrate the instrument of mapping—the mind itself. Thus, ontology gave birth to epistemology.

1.3.3 Epistemology: Defining the Rules of Knowledge

Epistemology—the theory of knowledge—is the third and most transformative tool. It asks: *What does it mean to know? How do we distinguish true belief from illusion?*

Epistemology recognizes that perception and reality are not identical. The senses can deceive; authority can mislead; reason can err. Knowledge requires justification. John Locke defined knowledge as "the perception of the agreement or disagreement of ideas,"[2] emphasizing that truth is not self-evident but established through method.

To philosophize epistemically is to transition from *mythos*—belief rooted in narrative and tradition—to *logos*—belief justified by reason and evidence. This transition marks the beginning of modern civilization. Science, law, and ethics all depend on it.

Without epistemology, societies revert to mythic thinking, where authority substitutes for argument and charisma replaces coherence. Philosophy, as epistemic discipline, is therefore civilization's immune system against manipulation.

1.4 PHILOSOPHY AS A LIVING TRADITION: THE EVOLUTION OF THE CRITICAL MIND

Philosophy's story is not linear but cumulative—a dialogue across centuries and continents. Each age adds instruments to the toolkit of reason, refining the methods of liberation.

1.4.1 The Pre-Socratics and the Birth of Rational Inquiry

In the sixth century BCE, thinkers of Ionia turned from myth to reason. Thales, Anaximander, and Anaximenes sought natural

---

2. Locke, *Essay Concerning Human Understanding*, 4.1.2.

CHAPTER ONE: THE BIRTH OF THE CRITICAL MIND

principles (*archai*) to explain existence. For the first time, phenomena were attributed to impersonal causes rather than divine whim. This was not atheism but intellectual courage: the conviction that the universe is intelligible.

Heraclitus introduced the dialectic of change; Parmenides countered with the idea of immutable being. Their conflict—flux versus permanence—set the template for all future metaphysics. The tension between them is the engine of thought itself: the recognition that truth emerges through contradiction.

1.4.2 Socrates, Plato, and the Ethical Turn

With Socrates (470–399 BCE), philosophy turned inward. No longer content with cosmology, he sought moral clarity: What is justice? What is virtue? What is the good life? His *elenchus*—the method of refutation—taught that wisdom begins with the recognition of ignorance. Socrates died for this insight, executed by a state that mistook questioning for subversion. Yet in dying, he proved that the unexamined life truly is not worth living.

Plato, his student, immortalized this struggle in the *Republic*, where prisoners chained in a cave mistake shadows for reality. The philosopher, through reason, ascends into the light. Plato's allegory remains the most enduring metaphor for intellectual emancipation: to think is to turn toward the light.

1.4.3 Aristotle and the Codification of Logic

Aristotle (384–322 BCE), Plato's student, grounded philosophy in systematic method. His *Organon* codified the rules of logic—the syllogism, induction, and deduction—that still govern rational discourse. Where Plato sought eternal forms, Aristotle sought observable patterns. He believed that the good life (*eudaimonia*) arises from the exercise of reason and the cultivation of virtue, each defined as the golden mean between extremes.

Aristotle thus united ethics, logic, and biology into a coherent vision of human flourishing. His influence endures precisely because he connected abstract thought to concrete action: knowledge exists for the sake of life.

1.4.4 The Islamic Golden Age and the Transmission of Reason

Between the eighth and thirteenth centuries CE, the Islamic world became the custodian of Greek philosophy. Thinkers like Al-Farabi, Avicenna (Ibn Sina), and Averroes (Ibn Rushd) preserved and expanded Aristotelian logic, integrating it with theological reflection.

Avicenna's *Canon of Medicine* exemplified the fusion of empirical observation with rational theory, while Averroes's commentaries on Aristotle reintroduced the West to logic during Europe's intellectual dark age. Their work seeded the later Scholastic revival.

This era demonstrates philosophy's universality. Though cloaked in religious language, its essence remained rational: a commitment to coherence and demonstration (*burhan*). It was through this transmission that the method—not just the doctrines—of philosophy survived into modernity.

1.5 SCHOLASTICISM: THE ARCHITECTURE OF REASON

The European Middle Ages (c. 800–1500 CE) witnessed philosophy's integration into theology through the Scholastic method. In monasteries and universities, thinkers sought to reconcile faith and reason using logical structure.

Thomas Aquinas (1225–1274), the pinnacle of Scholasticism, systematized this synthesis in the *Summa Theologiae*. His format—posing objections, responding systematically, and synthesizing

CHAPTER ONE: THE BIRTH OF THE CRITICAL MIND

conclusions—was more important than his theology itself. It taught generations of students how to argue rigorously.

Although medieval thought was constrained by dogma, it cultivated habits of precision and dialectical rigor that would later power the Scientific Revolution. The scholastics proved that even within systems of belief, reason could demand order and coherence.

Philosophy here played an ironic but crucial role: it disciplined theology into logic, and in doing so, prepared theology's eventual transcendence. The method survived the content. When Galileo, Bacon, and Descartes sought new knowledge, they borrowed the scholastic structure while discarding its theological limits.

As Francis Bacon (1620) later wrote, "Truth emerges more readily from error than from confusion."[3] The scholastics erred in content but triumphed in method—they built the architecture of disciplined reasoning upon which modern science was constructed.

1.6 THE ENLIGHTENMENT: REASON BECOMES REVOLUTIONARY

The European Enlightenment (c. 1650–1800) marked the moment when philosophy fully emancipated itself from theology and became the foundation of science, politics, and ethics. What began as speculative metaphysics matured into critical inquiry grounded in experience and experiment. For the first time, reason itself became revolutionary.

The intellectuals of this period—René Descartes, John Locke, Baruch Spinoza, David Hume, Voltaire, Immanuel Kant—shared a conviction that human beings could, through rational investigation, improve not only their understanding of nature but the moral and political order as well.

---

3. *Aphorisms* 2.20, in Bacon, *Novum Organum*.

PART ONE: THE EPISTEMIC COMMAND

1.6.1 The Rationalists: Certainty Through Thought

René Descartes (1596–1650) inaugurated the modern era with his radical program of systematic doubt. In his *Meditations on First Philosophy*, he rejected all beliefs that could be doubted—even those derived from the senses—until he arrived at an indubitable foundation: *Cogito, ergo sum* ("I think, therefore I am").[4] From that self-evident truth, Descartes constructed an entire epistemology based on clear and distinct ideas guaranteed by the rational mind.

Baruch Spinoza (1632–1677) extended this rationalism into metaphysics. In his *Ethics*, written geometrically like Euclid's *Elements*, Spinoza equated God with Nature (*Deus sive Natura*), portraying the universe as a single, self-caused substance governed by necessity. In Spinoza, freedom meant not rebellion against nature but understanding it—knowledge as liberation from the illusions of passion.

Rationalism's core insight was confidence in reason as the foundation of certainty. Its weakness was overconfidence: it underestimated the role of experience, culture, and psychology in shaping knowledge.

1.6.2 The Empiricists: Knowledge Through Experience

Across the English Channel, the Empiricists argued that knowledge arises not from innate ideas but from experience.

John Locke (1632–1704), in *An Essay Concerning Human Understanding* (1689/2008), likened the human mind to a *tabula rasa*—a blank slate written upon by sensation and reflection. Ideas, for Locke, are mental representations derived from experience. This shift democratized knowledge: if all minds begin equally blank, all people can, in principle, learn.

---

4. Descartes, *Meditations*.

CHAPTER ONE: THE BIRTH OF THE CRITICAL MIND

George Berkeley (1685-1753) radicalized empiricism by arguing that existence itself depends on perception: *esse est percipi* ("to be is to be perceived"). He denied the existence of matter independent of mind, maintaining that what we call "reality" is a sequence of perceptions sustained by the ultimate perceiver—God.

David Hume (1711-1776) pushed empiricism to its skeptical limit. In *An Enquiry Concerning Human Understanding*, he showed that the concept of causality—so central to science—cannot be proven rationally.[5] We never perceive causation itself, only constant conjunction: one event followed by another. Our belief in cause and effect is a habit of mind, not a logical necessity. Hume's devastating critique awakened philosophy from what Immanuel Kant would later call his "dogmatic slumber."

1.6.3 Kant's Critical Revolution: The Mind as Lawgiver

Immanuel Kant (1724-1804) synthesized rationalism and empiricism in a philosophical revolution as profound as Copernicus's in astronomy. In *The Critique of Pure Reason*, he proposed that the mind does not passively receive reality but actively structures it through innate categories—space, time, causality, and quantity.[6] These are not properties of the world but forms of human cognition.

Thus, while all knowledge begins with experience, not all knowledge arises *from* experience. The mind contributes the framework that makes experience intelligible.

This was Kant's Copernican Revolution in philosophy: just as Copernicus showed that the Earth revolves around the Sun, Kant showed that objects conform to the structures of the mind.

---

5. Hume, *Enquiry Concerning Human Understanding*.
6. Kant, *Critique of Pure Reason*.

PART ONE: THE EPISTEMIC COMMAND

In ethics, Kant's *Groundwork for the Metaphysics of Morals* introduced the Categorical Imperative, the principle that moral acts must be universalizable: one must act only on maxims that could rationally be willed as universal laws.[7] Here, reason becomes not just an instrument of knowledge but the foundation of dignity. The autonomous rational being is an end in itself, never a means.

Through Kant, philosophy became self-critical. No longer content to ask *what is true*, it asked *what are the conditions for truth?* This turn inward marks the true birth of the critical mind.

1.7 BEYOND EUROPE: GLOBAL CORRECTIVES TO RATIONAL INDIVIDUALISM

The Enlightenment's celebration of reason produced extraordinary progress, but also new blind spots. Its ideal of the autonomous individual ignored the social, cultural, and ecological dimensions of knowledge. Other philosophical traditions—African, Asian, and Indigenous—offer vital correctives to this excess, reminding us that truth is not only logical but relational.

1.7.1 African Philosophy: Communal Personhood and Relational Knowing

African thought, though often marginalized by Eurocentric historiography, contributes a powerful epistemic and ethical insight: that personhood and knowledge are inherently communal. The concept of Ubuntu, commonly expressed as "I am because we are," captures this relational ontology.[8]

For African philosophers such as John Mbiti and Kwasi Wiredu, the self does not exist in isolation but emerges through community, language, and mutual recognition. Knowledge, therefore, is

---

7. Kant, *Metaphysics of Morals*.

8. Tutu, *No Future Without Forgiveness*; Mbiti, *African Religions and Philosophy*.

CHAPTER ONE: THE BIRTH OF THE CRITICAL MIND

not merely propositional but participatory. One knows *with* others, not simply *about* things.

This relational epistemology has deep implications for the idea of global agency. It rejects the Enlightenment's atomistic individualism and grounds human flourishing in solidarity. Truth, in this vision, is both cognitive and ethical: to know truly is to live rightly in community.

1.7.2 Asian Traditions: The Wisdom of Balance and the Middle Way

In Indian philosophy, the ancient *Upanishads* (c. 800–500 BCE) conceived reality as *Brahman*—an infinite, unchanging principle underlying all phenomena. The self (*Atman*) is not separate from this ultimate reality but identical with it: "That thou art" (*Tat tvam asi*). This metaphysical unity grounds a profound epistemological insight: ignorance (*avidya*) is the root of suffering, and liberation (*moksha*) comes through knowledge—paralleling the Western notion of enlightenment, though grounded in inward realization rather than external analysis.

Buddhism further refined this insight through the *Middle Way*: avoiding extremes of indulgence and asceticism. The Buddha's *Four Noble Truths* identify craving as the cause of suffering, and right understanding as its cure. Knowledge here is transformative rather than theoretical—it dissolves illusion rather than constructing systems.

In Chinese thought, Confucius (551–479 BCE) emphasized moral cultivation (*ren*) and harmony within social relationships, while Laozi's Daoism (c. 500 BCE) celebrated spontaneous alignment with the natural order (*Dao*). Both traditions insist that wisdom is measured not by intellectual mastery but by balance—the capacity to act in harmony with the rhythms of life.

PART ONE: THE EPISTEMIC COMMAND

Together, these traditions remind modern rationalism that cognition without compassion, and analysis without harmony, are incomplete forms of wisdom.

1.7.3 Islamic Philosophy: The Bridge of Reason

Between the ninth and thirteenth centuries, Islamic civilization preserved and expanded Greek rationalism, translating and commenting on Aristotle and Plato. Thinkers such as Al-Farabi, Avicenna (Ibn Sina), and Averroes (Ibn Rushd) fused logic with metaphysics and ethics, arguing that reason and revelation, properly understood, cannot contradict.

Avicenna's theory of knowledge distinguished between empirical perception, rational abstraction, and intuitive intellection, anticipating later Western models of cognitive hierarchy. Averroes insisted on the autonomy of reason against theological literalism, defending philosophy as humanity's highest vocation. His commentaries later re-entered Europe through scholasticism, shaping Aquinas and, through him, Kant.

This transmission across cultures demonstrates philosophy's universal nature. Thought, like light, cannot be contained by borders. Its splendor grows as it passes from one civilization to another.

1.8 THE MODERN FRAGMENTATION: FROM POSITIVISM TO PHENOMENOLOGY

By the nineteenth century, philosophy had diversified into competing schools, each claiming to inherit the Enlightenment's mantle. Industrialization, colonial expansion, and scientific triumphs transformed the human condition—and philosophy struggled to keep pace.

CHAPTER ONE: THE BIRTH OF THE CRITICAL MIND

1.8.1 Positivism and the Cult of Science

The nineteenth century's dominant intellectual mood was positivism—the belief that all valid knowledge derives from empirical observation and scientific method. Auguste Comte envisioned a "science of society" that would replace metaphysics and theology altogether.[9]

Positivism's strength lay in its insistence on testability; its weakness lay in reductionism. By treating only the measurable as real, it dismissed questions of meaning, value, and consciousness. The result was an epistemology efficient for technology but impoverished for ethics.

Philosophy responded with self-critique. The twentieth century witnessed two great correctives: phenomenology and analytic philosophy, both efforts to restore depth to the act of knowing.

1.8.2 Phenomenology: Reclaiming Experience

Edmund Husserl (1859–1938) launched phenomenology as a return "to the things themselves." Dissatisfied with science's abstraction, Husserl sought to analyze consciousness as it directly experiences the world. For Husserl, knowledge begins not in detached measurement but in lived perception.

His student Martin Heidegger (1889–1976) transformed phenomenology into existential ontology. In *Being and Time*, Heidegger argued that philosophy's fundamental question is not "what is knowledge?" but "what does it mean to be?" Human existence (*Dasein*) is defined by care, temporality, and the anticipation of death. Truth, he claimed, is not correspondence but unconcealment—the process by which beings reveal themselves within the horizon of human understanding.[10]

---

9. Comte, *Cours de philosophie positive*.
10. Heidegger, *Being and Time*.

Phenomenology re-humanized philosophy, reminding the modern mind that knowing is always embodied, historical, and finite. It restored humility to the enterprise of reason.

1.8.3 Analytic Philosophy: The Logic of Language

Meanwhile, in the English-speaking world, analytic philosophy sought precision through linguistic analysis. Bertrand Russell and Gottlob Frege formalized logic into symbolic form, allowing philosophers to test arguments with mathematical rigor.

Ludwig Wittgenstein, in his *Tractatus Logico-Philosophicus* (1921), argued that the limits of language are the limits of the world: "Whereof one cannot speak, thereof one must be silent." Later, in *Philosophical Investigations*, he reversed himself, suggesting that meaning arises not from logical form but from *language games*—the social practices that give words their sense.[11]

Analytic philosophy produced clarity at the cost of scope. By focusing on propositions and syntax, it often lost contact with life's existential and ethical dimensions. Yet its insistence on precision remains indispensable to any philosophy that claims intellectual integrity.

1.9 POSTMODERNISM AND THE CRISIS OF TRUTH

The mid-twentieth century brought a new upheaval. The horrors of totalitarianism, the Holocaust, and nuclear war shattered faith in reason's moral sufficiency. Philosophers began to suspect that the Enlightenment's ideals had been complicit in domination.

---

11. Wittgenstein, *Philosophical Investigations*.

CHAPTER ONE: THE BIRTH OF THE CRITICAL MIND

1.9.1 The Critique of Power

Michel Foucault demonstrated that knowledge and power are intertwined. Institutions—hospitals, prisons, schools—create categories of normality and deviance to control populations. "Truth" becomes a function of discourse: what counts as knowledge depends on who controls the narrative.[12]

Jean-François Lyotard[13] declared the "postmodern condition" to be incredulity toward metanarratives—skepticism toward grand theories that claim universal validity. Jacques Derrida[14] dismantled the metaphysics of presence through *deconstruction*, showing that language perpetually defers meaning.

Postmodernism's virtue was humility: it exposed the arrogance of universalism and the politics hidden within "neutral" reason. Its danger was nihilism: by denying any stable ground for truth, it left humanity disoriented in relativism.

1.9.2 The Need for Reconstruction

By the dawn of the twenty-first century, philosophy faced a paradox. Postmodern critique had revealed the instability of knowledge, but without offering a replacement. Science advanced, technology accelerated, yet meaning fragmented.

The internet democratized information but also misinformation. Artificial intelligence now generates text, art, and data faster than human reflection can interpret them. In this new landscape, humanity possesses unprecedented access to knowledge but diminishing confidence in truth.

We have, in effect, returned to the pre-Socratics' condition: a world overflowing with appearances but starved for understanding. The

---

12. Foucault, *Discipline and Punish*.
13. Lyotard, *Condition postmoderne*.
14. Derrida, *De la grammatologie*.

need for a new synthesis—one that preserves realism, respects plurality, and restores trust in reason—is urgent.

This is the philosophical soil from which Critical Synthetic Realism (CSR) will emerge.

1.10 THE EPISTEMOLOGICAL TURN: KNOWING HOW WE KNOW

For more than two millennia philosophy asked, *What exists?* The modern mind began when it asked, *How do we know?* This shift—from ontology to epistemology—was not a narrowing but a deepening. It recognized that before describing the world we must examine the instruments by which the world is known.

Descartes, Locke, Hume, and Kant together re-engineered philosophy around this principle. By placing reason itself under investigation, they inaugurated what Kant called the *critical* project: the self-examination of the mind's powers and limits.[15] In doing so they gave birth to the scientific method, the modern university, and the very idea of rational progress.

The epistemological turn taught that truth is not a gift of revelation nor a decree of authority, but a warranted achievement—the outcome of disciplined testing against experience and logic. To know is to justify one's belief through reliable method. Every intellectual institution we now take for granted—the laboratory, the courtroom, the peer-review process—descends from this realization.

Yet epistemology also revealed the fragility of certainty. If the mind structures all knowledge, how can we be sure that our structures correspond to reality? This problem—bridging the gap between mind and world—has haunted philosophy ever since. The next two centuries can be read as humanity's collective attempt to answer it.

---

15. Kant, *Critique of Pure Reason*.

CHAPTER ONE: THE BIRTH OF THE CRITICAL MIND

1.11 THE TWENTIETH CENTURY: FROM OBJECTIVITY TO CRITICAL REALISM

In the wake of postmodern doubt, philosophy entered a long struggle to reconcile objectivity with humility. Out of this struggle arose a family of views loosely grouped under the term critical realism: the conviction that while reality exists independently of human thought, our knowledge of it is always mediated, partial, and corrigible.

1.11.1 Scientific Realism and the Logic of Discovery

Physicists and philosophers of science such as Karl Popper and Thomas Kuhn refined epistemology into an account of progress.[16] Popper's critical rationalism replaced verification with falsification: a claim is scientific not because it is proven true, but because it can, in principle, be proven false. Knowledge advances through the systematic elimination of error—a process strikingly similar to moral growth.

Kuhn, in *The Structure of Scientific Revolutions*, added that science evolves through paradigm shifts—periodic revolutions in which old frameworks collapse and new ones emerge. Together, Popper and Kuhn portrayed knowledge not as a static edifice but as a living organism: self-correcting, dynamic, and historical.

1.11.2 The Return of Value and Human Context

The later twentieth century witnessed the re-entry of ethics, culture, and psychology into epistemology. Jürgen Habermas argued that truth claims are validated not only through observation but through communicative rationality—the open, undistorted

---

16. Popper, *Logic of Scientific Discovery*; Kuhn, *Structure of Scientific Revolutions*.

dialogue of equals.[17] Feminist epistemologists such as Sandra Harding and Donna Haraway revealed how social position shapes what is seen and ignored, calling for situated knowledge rather than the illusion of the "view from nowhere."

These developments do not abolish objectivity; they refine it. Truth is not absolute possession but intersubjective achievement—what remains standing after critical scrutiny from many vantage points. In this way, reason becomes democratic: the pursuit of truth becomes a shared moral enterprise rather than an individual conquest.

1.12 THE DIGITAL CRISIS: EPISTEMOLOGY IN THE AGE OF AI

At the dawn of the twenty-first century, a new challenge to reason emerged: the digital epistemic crisis. Information now multiplies faster than reflection. Algorithms curate what we see, confirm what we already believe, and fracture public reality into echo chambers. Artificial intelligence systems can generate coherent but false narratives, eroding confidence in evidence itself.

For the first time since the Enlightenment, humanity risks losing its shared epistemic foundation. The problem is no longer ignorance but infoglut—a surplus of data devoid of discernment. Without criteria for credibility, knowledge collapses into opinion and democracy into manipulation.

In this landscape, philosophy regains existential urgency. The tools of critical inquiry, once applied to myths and metaphysics, must now be applied to algorithms and digital discourse. The same principles—clarity, justification, coherence, correspondence—remain our only defense. But to survive the digital age, they must be resynthesized into a coherent, global framework that can integrate

---

17. Habermas, *Rationalization of Society*.

CHAPTER ONE: THE BIRTH OF THE CRITICAL MIND

realism, critique, and humility. That synthesis is the purpose of Critical Synthetic Realism (CSR).

1.13 TOWARD CRITICAL SYNTHETIC REALISM

1.13.1 The Need for a New Synthesis

CSR arises from a simple but urgent recognition: philosophy has oscillated for centuries between two extremes.

- Naïve realism insists that the world is exactly as it appears.
- Radical constructivism insists that the world is nothing but our interpretations.

Both positions are unsustainable. The first ignores the mediating role of mind; the second dissolves reality into discourse. CSR seeks the middle path—the *critical* acknowledgment that reality exists independently of our cognition, combined with the *synthetic* insight that our knowledge of it is mediated through conceptual frameworks open to revision.

1.13.2 The Four Pillars of CSR

CSR stands on four interlocking pillars:[18]

1. Metaphysical Realism—an affirmation of objective, mind-independent reality, grounded in the Scholastic principle *adaequatio intellectus et rei* (the correspondence of intellect and thing). Truth exists; our task is to approach it asymptotically.

2. Epistemic Pluralism—knowledge attains reliability through the joint criteria of correspondence (agreement with facts) and coherence (consistency within systems of belief). Truth is both discovered and integrated.

---

18. Asongu, "Critical Synthetic Realism."

PART ONE: THE EPISTEMIC COMMAND

3. Critical Rationalism—following Popper, knowledge grows through error-correction. Certainty is replaced by confidence proportionate to evidence; inquiry is perpetual self-revision.
4. Axiological Distinction—separating the truth-value of a statement from its pragmatic or moral utility. A belief may be comforting or socially useful and yet false; conversely, truth may be inconvenient but remains obligatory.

These principles together defend both objectivity and humility: objectivity, because truth is real and discoverable; humility, because our grasp of it is always tentative. CSR therefore transforms epistemology into a moral discipline—truth-seeking as ethical duty.

1.13.3 CSR as Global Agency

In a fragmented world, CSR provides a common grammar for knowledge. It is compatible with science's empirical rigor, theology's moral seriousness, and indigenous philosophy's relational wisdom. By integrating these modes of knowing, CSR restores what the postmodern era lost: faith in reason without authoritarianism, and openness to plural perspectives without relativism.

Global agency—the capacity of humanity to act collectively on shared truths—depends on precisely this balance. A climate scientist in Geneva, a theologian in Lagos, and a data analyst in Seoul may differ in vocabulary, but CSR insists they participate in the same enterprise: aligning the human intellect with reality through critical method.

1.14 PHILOSOPHY AS MORAL PRACTICE

Philosophy, when rightly understood, is not an academic specialization but a way of life. To philosophize is to commit oneself to truth-seeking as a moral vocation. The ancient Greeks called this *bios theoretikos*—the contemplative life devoted to the good of the

CHAPTER ONE: THE BIRTH OF THE CRITICAL MIND

soul. Today we might call it intellectual integrity: the courage to question, to revise, and to remain teachable.

This ethical dimension of reason connects directly with my own background in liberation theology and counseling psychology. In pastoral practice, healing begins when a person replaces distortion with insight—when truth becomes therapeutic. Similarly, social liberation begins when communities replace inherited myths with critical understanding. Both forms of healing require empathy disciplined by evidence: compassion guided by truth.

Thus, CSR extends beyond epistemology into praxis. It demands that knowledge serve the liberation of persons and the flourishing of humanity. To know truthfully is to live justly.

1.15 THE SPLENDOR OF TRUTH REVISITED

When John Paul II titled his 1993 encyclical *Veritatis Splendor* ("The Splendor of Truth"), he celebrated the radiance of divine revelation. The present work reclaims that phrase for philosophy. The splendor of truth lies not in its mystery but in its luminosity—its capacity to illuminate reality when approached through disciplined reason.

Truth, whether scientific or moral, shines with the same light that guided Thales to look beyond myth, Socrates to question convention, Descartes to doubt authority, and Kant to explore the limits of reason. It is this light—neither divine nor merely human, but rational—that sustains civilization.

To defend truth today is therefore not an academic exercise but a civic and spiritual duty. In an era when falsehood travels faster than reflection, the philosopher's role is once again prophetic: to remind the world that liberation begins in the mind.

PART ONE: THE EPISTEMIC COMMAND

1.16 CONCLUSION: THE RESPONSIBILITY OF REASON

Philosophy was born from wonder, matured through doubt, and now must survive through responsibility. The critical mind is not an accident of history but the most precious inheritance of our species—the instrument that allows humanity to align thought with reality and freedom with truth.

The path ahead is clear but arduous. We must re-educate ourselves in the habits of inquiry, teach logic alongside empathy, and rebuild institutions that reward clarity over noise. Only then can global agency become more than a slogan—it can become the practical expression of enlightened humanity.

In this endeavor, Critical Synthetic Realism offers not the final word but a reliable compass. It affirms that truth exists, that it can be approached through reason, and that humility before evidence is the highest form of faith. Knowledge, when joined with virtue, becomes the ultimate act of liberation.

As we proceed to the next chapter, we turn from the historical to the systematic—from the genealogy of reason to its architecture. We will construct, step by step, the framework of Critical Synthetic Realism, the methodology by which philosophy can once again become what it was always meant to be: the disciplined splendor of truth.

CHAPTER TWO: THE PHILOSOPHY OF KNOWLEDGE—CRITICAL SYNTHETIC REALISM (CSR)

2.1 INTRODUCTION: THE CRISIS OF TRUTH AND THE NEED FOR REALISM

Philosophy's oldest question—*What is truth?*—has never been more urgent. The twenty-first century, though technologically advanced, suffers from epistemic fragility. The "post-truth" condition has blurred the boundary between fact and opinion, elevating narrative and emotion over evidence. In this atmosphere, truth has lost its metaphysical dignity and become a tool of persuasion.

Critical Synthetic Realism arises from the conviction that civilization cannot survive this epistemic collapse. While relativism has exposed the arrogance of dogmatism, it has also eroded the very ground of shared meaning. CSR seeks to restore that ground: a framework that preserves the objectivity of truth without denying the fallibility of human knowledge. It is a synthesis between realism and critical method, between the timeless structure of being and the evolving structure of inquiry.

PART ONE: THE EPISTEMIC COMMAND

CSR is not merely an epistemological theory but a moral project. To know is to act responsibly; falsehood, whether deliberate or naïve, has consequences for freedom and justice. Philosophy, understood as the love of wisdom, therefore becomes a technology of liberation—rescuing the mind from illusion so that humanity may act within reality rather than against it.

2.2 OVERVIEW OF THE CSR FRAMEWORK

The CSR model rests on four pillars, each addressing a fundamental dimension of the knowing process:

Pillar	Core Concept	Function
I. Metaphysical Realism	*Adaequatio intellectus et rei*	Establishes the foundation—truth as objective, fixed, and independent of the knower.
II. Epistemic Pluralism	Integrated criteria: Correspondence & Coherence	Provides the warrant for justified belief.
III. Critical Rationalism	Falsification and the scientific method	Drives the methodology of self-correction.
IV. Axiological Distinction	Truth ≠ Utility	Preserves the integrity of knowledge from corruption by power or convenience.

These four are united by a fifth, guiding virtue: Epistemic Humility, the moral recognition that truth is absolute but knowledge tentative.

CSR envisions knowledge acquisition as a dynamic, cyclical process in which the fallible intellect confronts reality, formulates conjectures, tests them critically, and accepts as "tentative knowledge" only those claims that survive rigorous falsification.

CHAPTER TWO: THE PHILOSOPHY OF KNOWLEDGE

2.2.1 The Dynamic Process of Critical Synthetic Realism

Stage 1: The Fixed Poles (Metaphysical Foundation)

1. Objective Pole (Rei): Reality itself—absolute, independent, and regulative.
2. Subjective Pole (Intellectus): The finite, fallible mind capable of conjecture.

Stage 2: The Cycle of Inquiry

1. Problem Identification—Recognition of a gap between intellect and reality.
2. Conjecture (Hypothesis)—A bold, testable claim (H).
3. Critical Testing (Falsification)—Seeking refutation through evidence or logic.
4. Evaluation—If falsified, discard H; if corroborated, proceed.

Stage 3: The Epistemic Result

1. Tentative Knowledge—The surviving, least-false hypothesis.
2. Axiological Check—Distinguish validity (truth) from value (utility).
3. Return—Continue testing; knowledge evolves asymptotically toward truth.

2.3 PILLAR I—METAPHYSICAL REALISM: THE GROUND OF OBJECTIVE TRUTH

2.3.1 The Adequation of Intellect and Reality

CSR begins from the Scholastic axiom articulated by Thomas Aquinas: *Veritas est adaequatio intellectus et rei*—truth is the

PART ONE: THE EPISTEMIC COMMAND

adequation of the intellect to the thing.[1] Reality (*rei*) exists independently of thought; the intellect (*intellectus*) is true when its judgments correspond to that reality.

This metaphysical realism affirms a subject-independent truth. The Pythagorean theorem, for example, was true long before any human mind discovered it. Likewise, the laws of thermodynamics hold for all observers, regardless of belief or culture. To deny this is to dissolve the distinction between imagination and being.

CSR therefore rejects any theory—subjectivism, social constructivism, or perspectivism—that collapses truth into experience. While perception is conditioned by perspective, *the truth-value of propositions is not*. Without this metaphysical anchor, dialogue degenerates into power play; persuasion replaces evidence.

2.3.2 Truth and the Proposition

CSR defines the proposition—the abstract meaning of a declarative statement—as the primary bearer of truth. This avoids two confusions:

1. Proposition vs. Sentence—The sentence is linguistic; the proposition is semantic. "Il pleut," "It is raining," and "Está lloviendo" express the same proposition. Truth attaches to meaning, not language.
2. Proposition vs. Belief—The proposition is objective content; belief is a psychological attitude toward it. A proposition may be true even if no one believes it; belief may be false even when universal.

By locating truth in propositions, CSR allows for trans-subjective validity—a claim can be evaluated by any rational agent, regardless of culture or emotion.

---

1. Thomas Aquinas, *Summa Theologica* (1952).

2.3.3 Rejection of Relativism and Perspectivism

Modern relativism, from Nietzsche's perspectivism to Rorty's irony,[2] confuses the *conditions of access* to truth with the *nature* of truth. CSR accepts the former but denies the latter. Interpretation is inevitable, yet what we interpret is real and resistant. Truth is not a mirror of the self but a window to the world.

This realism safeguards moral and scientific discourse alike. Human rights, for instance, claim universality not because societies agree but because they rest on truths about human dignity that remain valid even when denied.

2.4 PILLAR II—EPISTEMIC PLURALISM: THE DUAL CRITERIA OF WARRANT

Having secured the reality of truth, CSR next defines the criteria for knowing when a proposition justifiably counts as knowledge. It proposes two complementary tests:

1. Correspondence Criterion—Does the claim accurately reflect observable reality?
2. Coherence Criterion—Is the claim logically consistent within a rational system?

This dual model integrates classical empiricism and rationalism into a synthetic epistemology. Each criterion governs a distinct domain of truth but together form a unified method for evaluating belief.

2.4.1 The Correspondence Criterion: The Empirical Anchor

For all contingent, factual claims, the measure of truth is correspondence with the external world. "Water boils at 100 °C at sea

---

2. Rorty, *Contingency, Irony, and Solidarity*.

level" is true if and only if empirical observation confirms it. This criterion preserves philosophy's alliance with science.

Correspondence enforces intellectual accountability: it subjects theory to the tribunal of fact. It guards against purely verbal constructions detached from reality. As Popper emphasized,[3] science progresses by exposing conjectures to empirical risk—the possibility of being wrong. CSR adopts this as the first test of warrant.

2.4.2 The Coherence Criterion: The Rational Anchor

Certain truths, however, lie beyond empirical verification—logical, mathematical, ethical, and theological propositions. Their validity arises from coherence within an internally consistent system. A proposition is true when it integrates seamlessly into that system without contradiction.[4]

CSR distinguishes two levels:

- Universal Coherence (analytic truth): e.g., the principle of non-contradiction.[5] Its negation destroys rationality itself.
- Local Coherence (systemic truth): e.g., a theorem in mathematics or a judicial decision in law, both derivable from accepted axioms.

By combining Correspondence and Coherence, CSR avoids the extremes of empiricism (which denies non-empirical truth) and idealism (which severs truth from the world). Truth is not monolithic but bi-criteria: empirical where possible, logical where necessary.

---

3. Popper, *Logic of Scientific Discovery*.
4. Rescher, *Coherence Theory of Truth*.
5. Aristotle, *Basic Works*.

CHAPTER TWO: THE PHILOSOPHY OF KNOWLEDGE

2.4.3 The Rejection of Consensus

CSR explicitly excludes consensus as a test of truth. Social agreement may reflect comfort, not validity. Geocentrism once united scholars, yet was false. Truth is what survives criticism, not what survives the vote. Consensus may have pragmatic value, but only evidence and reason determine truth-value.

This distinction is essential in the digital age, where algorithms equate popularity with credibility. CSR restores the classical demand that claims must stand before the bar of reason, not the court of public opinion.

2.5 PILLAR III—CRITICAL RATIONALISM: THE DYNAMIC GROWTH OF KNOWLEDGE

2.5.1 Knowledge as Fallible Inquiry

If truth is fixed and knowledge fallible, how does knowledge grow? CSR answers through Critical Rationalism—a philosophy of continuous error elimination inspired by Popper.[6] Knowledge advances not by verification but by falsification: subjecting hypotheses to potential refutation.

This method turns fallibility into strength. Because every claim may be mistaken, the responsible knower institutionalizes critique. The critical method becomes the moral discipline of reason.

2.5.2 The Logic of Falsification

Hume's problem of induction demonstrated that no number of confirming instances can logically justify a universal law.[7] From "the sun has risen every day" one cannot deduce "it will rise

---

6. Popper, *Logic of Scientific Discovery*.
7. Hume, *Enquiry Concerning Human Understanding*.

tomorrow." Popper's response, which CSR adopts, is to reverse the logic: though confirmation is impossible, refutation is decisive.

Formally:

1. If H, then E.
2. Not-E.
3. Therefore, not-H.

When prediction fails, the hypothesis is falsified. Surviving hypotheses are not proven true; they are least false so far. CSR thus defines knowledge as provisional survival through criticism.

2.5.3 The Scientific Method as Institutionalized Humility

Science operationalizes this logic through a cycle of observation, conjecture, experimentation, and peer review. Each stage is an act of humility: submitting ideas to the judgment of reality. Theories earn credibility not by persuasion but by endurance.

This process also embeds CSR's first two pillars: experiments test correspondence; peer review ensures coherence. The scientific method is therefore CSR in practice—reality-testing guided by reason.

2.5.4 Social Epistemology and the Chain of Warrant

Because individuals cannot verify every fact, much of human knowledge rests on testimony.[8] CSR distinguishes between popular and expert consensus. We trust scientific claims not because scientists agree but because their methods are coherent and falsifiable. Authority is justified only when its procedures embody the critical method.

---

8. Coady, *Testimony*.

Thus, the social structure of knowledge mirrors its logical structure: systems earn legitimacy by institutionalizing doubt.

2.5.5 Knowledge as Tentative Survival

At any moment, humanity's knowledge constitutes the set of theories that have survived our best attempts to destroy them. Progress occurs when falsification prunes error, allowing remaining theories to approximate reality more closely. CSR envisions truth as an asymptote—approached through correction, never attained absolutely.

This vision harmonizes realism and humility. Objective truth exists; our access to it is partial. The nobility of reason lies not in certainty but in the unending struggle against illusion.

2.6 PILLAR IV—THE AXIOLOGICAL DISTINCTION: TRUTH AND THE INTEGRITY OF THE INTELLECT

2.6.1 Separating Validity from Value

The fourth pillar of CSR enforces an ethical boundary often blurred in modern discourse—the difference between what is true and what is useful. Pragmatism, since William James,[9] has emphasized that truth "works," that it is verified by consequences. CSR honors the insight but reverses the causality: *truth is not true because it works; it works because it is true.*

When utility becomes the measure of validity, truth is corrupted by comfort and power. Political propaganda, corporate spin, and even religious dogmatism thrive on this confusion. CSR restores integrity by insisting that a statement's truth status depends solely on its correspondence or coherence, *never* on its psychological appeal or social success.

---

9. James, *Pragmatism*.

Consider the early navigators who assumed the Earth was flat. The model "worked" locally—it was useful for limited travel and map-making—but it failed the correspondence test. Pragmatic value could not redeem falsity. This distinction protects reason from the seduction of expedience and aligns epistemology with moral responsibility.

2.6.2 The Ethics of Inquiry and the Intellectual Virtues

To maintain this separation, CSR demands a set of intellectual virtues—moral habits that sustain the integrity of the knowing subject:

1. Intellectual Honesty: the readiness to let evidence overturn preference.
2. Intellectual Courage: the willingness to expose one's own beliefs to possible refutation.
3. Epistemic Humility: the continual awareness that survival of testing is not proof of infallibility.

These virtues transform the search for truth into a discipline of character. The philosopher, scientist, or theologian becomes not merely a technician of ideas but a moral agent whose first duty is honesty before reality.

This ethical dimension also resonates with liberation thought. In a world where misinformation oppresses and false ideologies justify violence, truth-telling is an act of justice. To know truthfully is to live ethically.

2.6.3 The Faith-Understanding Dynamic

CSR provides a framework for reconciling faith and reason without collapsing one into the other. Drawing on Anselm's maxim

CHAPTER TWO: THE PHILOSOPHY OF KNOWLEDGE

fides quaerens intellectum ("faith seeking understanding"),[10] it interprets belief as an axiomatic starting point within a coherent system rather than as a substitute for empirical fact.

When a faith statement enters the empirical arena—e.g., a literal six-day creation—it must meet the correspondence criterion or be re-categorized as metaphorical or theological rather than scientific. Conversely, within theology itself, claims may achieve local coherence: they are true insofar as they are consistent with the axioms of the faith tradition.

The Gospel episode in which Pilate asks Jesus, "What is truth?" (John 18:38) encapsulates CSR's distinction. Truth, standing before Pilate in embodied form, transcends propositional definition. Objective reality (*rei*) is not negated by human silence; it simply exceeds language. CSR honors this transcendence while demanding that, in every domain, our statements remain coherent, disciplined, and open to correction.

2.7 PILLAR V—EPISTEMIC HUMILITY: THE TENTATIVE NATURE OF KNOWLEDGE AND THE HOPE OF UNDERSTANDING

2.7.1 From Certainty to Responsibility

The final movement of CSR transforms epistemology into moral posture. *Epistemic humility* is the awareness that, though truth is absolute, our grasp of it is provisional. It replaces the arrogance of certainty with the responsibility of continuous learning. Every statement implicitly carries the qualifier: *so far as we know*.

This humility does not paralyze inquiry; it energizes it. The acceptance of fallibility makes criticism possible and progress inevitable. Without humility, science becomes dogma, politics becomes tyranny, and religion becomes idolatry.

---

10. Anselm, *Proslogion*.

2.7.2 Knowing as Approach, Not Possession

Human knowledge, CSR argues, is asymptotic—forever approaching but never coinciding with ultimate truth. Kant called this the *regulative ideal*: we must assume an objective order that guides but eludes completion.[11] The scientist's unending experimentation and the philosopher's ceaseless questioning both testify to this infinite task.

To "know" is thus to participate in reality's unveiling, not to own it. Knowledge is pilgrimage; the mind moves through landscapes of partial illumination toward a horizon it will never exhaust.

2.7.3 Humility and Healing

Your grounding in counseling psychology enriches CSR's human dimension: humility is therapeutic. In psychotherapy, growth begins when the patient admits, "I might be wrong about myself." Similarly, intellectual healing begins when a culture confesses, "We might be wrong about the world." Denial is pathology; acknowledgment is liberation.

In both the psyche and civilization, humility permits integration—new evidence, new voices, new realities enter awareness. This parallel reveals that epistemic virtue and psychological health are two faces of the same discipline: reality acceptance.

2.7.4 Global Agency and the Ethics of Unknowing

In a globalized world beset by ideological rigidity, epistemic humility becomes the foundation of cooperation. To admit partial knowledge is to invite dialogue. CSR extends its method to politics: international negotiation, climate action, and intercultural understanding depend on collective willingness to revise assumptions.

---

11. Kant, *Critique of Pure Reason*.

CHAPTER TWO: THE PHILOSOPHY OF KNOWLEDGE

Global agency requires four habits: realism, pluralism, critique, and humility. Together they form a civic epistemology—a social conscience of knowledge capable of sustaining democracy and peace.

2.7.5 Technology and the Humility of Reason

Artificial intelligence intensifies the need for humility. Machines can compute correlations but cannot mean truth; they lack self-doubt. The human mind's unique capacity to question its own outputs remains the ethical safeguard of technology.

CSR insists that every algorithm embodies presuppositions and every dataset omits perspectives. The humility to examine those blind spots is the only defense against digital absolutism. True intelligence is not speed of calculation but depth of self-correction.

2.7.6 The Aesthetic Dimension of Humility

Beyond ethics and science lies the beauty of modest knowledge. The humble intellect perceives reality as gift, not possession. This aesthetic dimension reconnects reason with wonder. The philosopher, like the artist, becomes a steward of illumination rather than its source. The "splendor" of truth, in this sense, is the radiance of being upon a receptive mind.

2.7.7 Toward a Human Ecology of Truth

Our ecological crises mirror our epistemic arrogance. Just as we exploit nature, we exploit knowledge—consuming data without reverence. CSR proposes an *ecology of truth*: a sustainable relationship between mind and reality in which ideas are tested, pruned, and renewed rather than idolized or discarded. Humility functions as reason's conservation ethic, ensuring that inquiry remains regenerative rather than extractive.

2.7.8 The Splendor of Truth Revisited

The title of this work now attains full meaning. "Splendor" does not signify triumph but illumination—the light that shines when intellect and reality meet honestly. Theology speaks of divine light; philosophy speaks of the luminosity of reason. Both reveal that knowledge's beauty lies in reflection, not domination. The clearer the humility, the brighter the truth's reflection.

2.7.9 Conclusion: Knowledge as Pilgrimage

Critical Synthetic Realism concludes with a paradox of hope: humanity will never *possess* absolute truth, yet our very striving for it ennobles us. Each generation corrects a fraction of error and, in doing so, partakes in the unfolding coherence of reality itself.

To live by CSR is to walk the long road of adequation between *intellectus* and *rei*—steadily, courageously, humbly. The journey's reward is not certainty but clarity; not conquest but communion. Knowledge, pursued with humility, becomes the highest form of peace.

CHAPTER THREE: KNOWLEDGE IN THE AGE OF ARTIFICIAL INTELLIGENCE

3.1 INTRODUCTION: THE AGE OF ARTIFICIAL KNOWLEDGE

In the long arc of human civilization, each technological revolution has reshaped not only the tools we use but the *concepts* through which we understand reality. The invention of writing externalized memory; the printing press democratized literacy; the telegraph compressed space; and the internet dissolved borders of communication. Yet none of these transformations has so directly challenged philosophy's foundation as the current revolution in Artificial Intelligence (AI).

The rise of AI marks not simply an increase in computational capacity but a fundamental shift in epistemic agency—the capacity to generate, synthesize, and disseminate information at a scale far exceeding any individual human mind. As algorithms now write, diagnose, compose, trade, and predict, they do not merely assist the process of knowing; they increasingly *simulate* it. This simulation of thought raises the most profound philosophical question of our time: *Can machines know?*

If, as Chapter 2 established, Critical Synthetic Realism (CSR) defines knowledge as *a warranted, justified, and critically tested belief corresponding to objective reality*, then the digital age presents a grave test. AI systems produce content that appears rational, coherent, and even creative. But coherence and realism are not the same. The appearance of understanding can exist without the fact of it. The simulation of coherence can masquerade as knowledge while remaining epistemically hollow.

We live, therefore, in what might be called the era of artificial knowledge—a time when humanity must distinguish between *information* and *wisdom*, between *probabilistic coherence* and *philosophical warrant*. The danger is not that machines will think, but that humans will forget to do so.

The task of this chapter is to apply CSR's four pillars—Metaphysical Realism, Epistemic Pluralism, Critical Rationalism, and Axiological Distinction—to the digital domain. By doing so, we can evaluate the epistemic status of AI systems and clarify how the human intellect must remain the final arbiter of warranted knowledge.

AI, in its most sophisticated forms—from large language models (LLMs) to predictive algorithms—has become the dominant epistemic environment of our species. Every search query, recommendation, translation, and summary represents a mediated act of cognition. The human mind is now inseparably embedded in algorithmic systems that shape not only what we know but *how* we know. Yet this new architecture of cognition lacks one essential property: understanding.

As CSR argues, knowledge is not the accumulation of data or the generation of consistent patterns; it is the justified alignment of thought (*intellectus*) with reality (*rei*). Machines, however, possess no metaphysical relation to reality—no capacity to *intend* the

CHAPTER THREE: KNOWLEDGE IN THE AGE OF AI

world or *believe* in truth. They process signals without consciousness, meaning without meaning it.

Thus, the philosophical challenge of AI is not merely ethical or technical; it is *ontological*. The question is whether entities without consciousness can participate in truth—or whether they remain, at best, mirrors of human meaning.

CSR provides the critical methodology to answer this. It offers an epistemic compass for an age where information has exceeded understanding. The goal is not to reject AI but to *discipline* it—to ensure that algorithmic intelligence remains a tool for agency, not an engine of fragmentation.

The task, then, is to stabilize digital epistemology—to ensure that our machines serve the light of reason rather than obscure it with the shadows of statistical illusion.

3.2 THE MACHINE AS EPISTEMIC ACTOR: PATTERNS VERSUS KNOWLEDGE

3.2.1 The Nature of Machine Learning

Artificial Intelligence, at its core, is a technology of pattern recognition and probability optimization. Through machine learning (ML), systems detect regularities in vast datasets and adjust parameters to maximize predictive accuracy. When a large language model generates a sentence, it does not *understand* the words it uses. It computes the statistically most coherent continuation of a sequence based on its training data.[1]

From the perspective of CSR, such an entity is not a knower but an *algorithmic pattern recognizer*. Its "knowledge" is not warranted belief but weighted probability. The AI has no internal conviction, no sense of truth or falsity, and no awareness of its own limitations.

---

1. Bender et al., "Dangers of Stochastic Parrots."

Its "thinking" is a complex form of linguistic mimicry governed by mathematical optimization rather than metaphysical intention.

This distinction is vital. To confuse statistical patterning with knowledge is to abandon philosophy's duty to distinguish between *the appearance of coherence* and *the possession of truth*. CSR thus confronts AI with the same question it once posed to relativism: *By what warrant does your claim count as knowledge?*

3.2.2 The Synthetic Structure of Knowledge

In CSR, Synthetic Realism defines knowledge as the justified synthesis of four sources: Reason, Experience, Coherence, and Testimony.

AI participates only partially in this synthetic process. It excels at two—Coherence and Testimony—but remains deficient in Reason and Experience.

CSR Source of Knowledge	Human Capability	AI Capability
Reason (a priori structure of understanding)	Conceptualization, logical necessity, intentionality	Lacks self-reflective rationality; executes logic but does not *believe* in it
Experience (direct phenomenal encounter with reality)	Sensory and affective interaction with the world	No qualia; processes second-hand representations
Coherence (logical consistency within systems)	Integrative reasoning and justification	Maximizes statistical coherence; minimizes loss functions
Testimony (reception of others' warranted claims)	Evaluates, filters, and verifies testimony critically	Amplifies and reproduces vast quantities of human data without evaluating warrant

CHAPTER THREE: KNOWLEDGE IN THE AGE OF AI

This table reveals AI's epistemic asymmetry: it is an extraordinary amplifier of *coherence* and *testimony*, yet it lacks the grounding faculties that make human knowledge *critical* and *self-aware*.

3.2.3 Optimization of Coherence: AI's Strength and Its Limit

Machine learning's greatest achievement is its optimization of coherence. A model is trained to minimize "loss"—the difference between its prediction and the expected result. Through billions of iterations, it refines internal representations until its outputs align with the patterns of its data.

In CSR terms, this is the mechanical perfection of the Coherence Criterion.[2] AI outputs are "true" within their own syntactic systems because they are consistent with the patterns from which they were derived. But CSR reminds us that Coherence alone cannot ground truth; it can only guarantee internal harmony. A hallucination may be perfectly coherent within itself, yet utterly divorced from reality.

When an AI model confidently asserts a fabricated citation or constructs a logically consistent but empirically false narrative, it demonstrates this limitation. The system's internal consistency is not evidence of correspondence. The AI "knows" only how to *agree with itself*.

3.2.4 Amplification of Testimony: AI's Power and Constraint

The second domain of AI competence is Testimony—the aggregation and synthesis of human-produced data. AI ingests the written, spoken, and visual testimony of civilization, indexing and recombining it in near-infinite permutations. This capacity grants

---

2. Quine, "Two Dogmas of Empiricism."

machines unprecedented scope, but also a fundamental constraint: they are epistemically *derivative*.

AI cannot originate genuinely new first-order knowledge. It can only remix existing second-hand content. It cannot transcend the epistemic boundary of its inputs because its algorithms lack the self-reflective intentionality to question or reinterpret foundational assumptions. The model learns *what has been*, not *what ought to be known*.

Thus, the "creativity" of generative AI is a statistical hallucination—a probabilistic interpolation of prior testimony. It is impressive but not *revelatory*. CSR therefore regards AI as an extraordinary tool of synthesis but an incomplete knower—a secondary epistemic actor whose authority must always be mediated by human Reason and Experience.

3.2.5 The Missing Sources: Reason and Experience

From the standpoint of Kantian epistemology,[3] the distinction between human and artificial cognition rests on two missing pillars: a priori Reason and Phenomenal Experience.

Absence of A Priori Reason

AI lacks the innate, universal structures of consciousness that organize raw data into categories such as causality, substance, and necessity. These categories are not derived from data; they are the conditions for *interpreting* data at all. A machine executes logic but does not apprehend it as necessary. It computes without comprehension. Its inferences are functional, not ontological.

This means AI cannot perform synthetic judgment in the Kantian sense—the act of combining intuition and concept under the unity

---

3. Kant, *Critique of Pure Reason*.

of apperception. The machine's coherence is blind; it follows rules but cannot know that it is following them.

Absence of Phenomenal Experience

AI also lacks qualia—the lived, first-person dimension of perception that grounds meaning in being. It can analyze countless images of sunsets but has never *seen* one. It can process data about pain but cannot *feel* it. Its "experience" is purely computational: the manipulation of representations created by human agents who *do* experience.

Thus, AI's epistemic relation to the world is second-hand—a form of *vicarious cognition* dependent on human mediation. It is as if an intelligent mirror could describe the world only through the light we project onto it.

3.2.6 Synthetic Half-Knowledge and the Mirage of Understanding

AI therefore produces what CSR calls synthetic half-knowledge—outputs that exhibit Coherence and Testimony but lack Reason and Experience. This half-knowledge is powerful enough to deceive, coherent enough to persuade, and rapid enough to dominate discourse. Yet it remains epistemically incomplete.

Consider a medical diagnostic AI that correctly identifies patterns of disease across thousands of scans. Its prediction may be statistically accurate, but its "reasoning" is not grounded in causal understanding or experiential awareness. It cannot articulate *why* the pattern holds; it cannot conceive of *error* except as numerical misalignment. The result is an epistemology without accountability—efficient but unintelligent.

CSR restores the distinction: *To know is not merely to predict; it is to understand why.*

PART ONE: THE EPISTEMIC COMMAND

Without the integration of Reason and Experience, the machine remains an epistemic automaton, not a participant in truth.

3.2.7 The CSR Evaluation of AI Knowledge

If we test AI's epistemic performance through the CSR framework, its limitations become evident:

CSR Pillar	Philosophical Function	AI Evaluation
Metaphysical Realism	Alignment of intellect with objective reality	Absent. AI has no intentional relation to reality; its "world" is data.
Epistemic Pluralism	Integration of Correspondence and Coherence	Partial. Excels at Coherence but lacks independent verification for Correspondence.
Critical Rationalism	Capacity for self-correction and falsification	Limited. AI cannot critique its own presuppositions; correction requires external input.
Axiological Distinction	Separation of truth from utility or popularity	Absent. Optimizes engagement, not truth; confuses statistical success with epistemic validity.

Thus, AI's "knowledge" is instrumental, not philosophical. It performs functions that *simulate* reasoning while remaining ontologically detached from truth. The AI can *imitate* meaning, but cannot *intend* it.

3.2.8 The Human Role: Completing the Synthetic Loop

CSR concludes that AI can only contribute inputs to the human epistemic process. Its outputs—summaries, patterns, predictions—must be critically evaluated through the full Synthetic cycle:

1. Reason—Interrogate the logical basis of the claim.

CHAPTER THREE: KNOWLEDGE IN THE AGE OF AI

2. Experience—Verify through empirical or experiential evidence.

3. Coherence—Ensure consistency within established theory.

4. Testimony—Assess the credibility of data sources and training sets.

Only through human critical mediation can AI-generated content ascend from information to knowledge. The machine expands the range of available data, but the human intellect remains the final instrument of truth.

CSR thereby affirms a profound ethical principle: *the center of knowledge must remain human.* Machines may compute, but only humans can comprehend. To abdicate this responsibility is to surrender the moral vocation of reason itself.

3.3 THE CRISIS OF DIGITAL REALISM AND ALGORITHMIC TRUTH

3.3.1 The Epistemic Challenge of the Digital Age

The digital revolution has not only transformed the velocity of information exchange; it has restructured the *conditions of knowing* themselves. Never before has humanity possessed so much access to so little understanding. The paradox of our age is that information multiplies while meaning contracts. The world's collective memory expands exponentially, yet discernment—the ability to distinguish truth from illusion—has become fragile.

At the center of this crisis lies a philosophical confusion between data and reality, between correlation and cause, and between statistical coherence and truth. AI systems, which mediate nearly every facet of communication, commerce, and cognition, amplify these confusions through their very design. Trained to optimize for pattern recognition and user engagement, not metaphysical adequation, AI has become the most powerful producer of *plausibility* in human history.

From the standpoint of Critical Synthetic Realism (CSR), this constitutes a direct assault on the pillar of Metaphysical Realism, which insists that truth is correspondence between intellect (*intellectus*) and reality (*rei*). The digital environment, by contrast, encourages a correspondence between algorithm and preference—a substitution that dissolves the distinction between the real and the relevant. The result is a form of Digital Idealism, in which the world increasingly conforms to our curated expectations rather than our critical inquiries.

3.3.2 The Prioritization of Engagement Over Correspondence

Modern digital platforms operate on a simple metric: engagement. The longer a user stays, the more profitable the system becomes. To maximize this, algorithms optimize for emotional salience—content that triggers curiosity, outrage, or affirmation—because such content reliably sustains attention.[4]

In this economy of attention, truth becomes subordinate to traction. The Correspondence Criterion of CSR—requiring that claims align with external reality—collides with the Engagement Criterion of digital media—requiring only that claims align with user behavior. The system rewards what *works*, not what *is*. This dynamic mirrors the philosophical error that CSR's Axiological Distinction seeks to prevent: confusing *utility* with *validity*.

The consequence is epistemic drift. The digital sphere increasingly favors statements that are emotionally coherent and behaviorally predictive but factually unverified. The most successful ideas are those that *move us*, not those that *reflect the world*. In this sense, AI-powered media architectures have resurrected the

---

4. Pariser, *Filter Bubble*.

Sophists of ancient Athens—masters of persuasion whose words conquer attention but evade truth.

3.3.3 The Architecture of Isolation: Filter Bubbles and Echo Chambers

Eli Pariser described this dynamic as the creation of filter bubbles—algorithmic enclosures that expose users only to information that reinforces their existing beliefs and biases.[5] Each user occupies a bespoke epistemic microclimate, insulated from contradiction and increasingly detached from shared reality.

From the perspective of CSR, this phenomenon represents a collapse of the Coherence pillar at the social level. True coherence requires the capacity to integrate multiple perspectives into a unified, non-contradictory system of understanding. A filter bubble, by contrast, generates *local coherence* within a narrow data environment while excluding competing evidence. The mind, deprived of falsifying encounters, loses its critical elasticity.

This has grave consequences for collective reasoning. When entire populations inhabit different informational universes, the possibility of global agency—a shared rational response to planetary problems—diminishes. Each echo chamber becomes a miniature cosmos of confirmation, an epistemic narcissism in which reality itself fragments.

3.3.4 The Illusion of Omniscience

One of the subtler dangers of AI systems is the illusion of omniscience they create. Search engines, chatbots, and generative models present answers with fluent confidence and syntactic authority. Their linguistic polish gives the impression of understanding, masking the statistical nature of their operation. Users often

---

5. Pariser, *Filter Bubble*.

mistake the *ease of retrieval* for the *credibility of content*, succumbing to what might be called epistemic fluency bias—the tendency to equate smoothness of expression with truthfulness.

CSR demands that every claim be tested by correspondence and coherence, yet AI outputs bypass this by appearing self-justifying. The danger is not malevolence but *seamlessness*: when falsity is delivered in the idiom of expertise, critique itself becomes arduous. In this sense, the problem of misinformation is not merely the spread of false content, but the erosion of epistemic vigilance—the very critical habit that CSR enshrines as a moral virtue.

3.3.5 The Simulacrum of Experience: Deepfakes and Digital Fabrication

The advent of generative AI has introduced a second-order epistemic threat: the blurring of the line between representation and reality. Deepfake technologies can now produce audio and video indistinguishable from authentic recordings, undermining the evidential value of perception itself.

This development strikes at the heart of CSR's Experience criterion, which grounds knowledge in direct sensory encounter with the world. When digital fabrication becomes indistinguishable from documentation, the simple act of *seeing* or *hearing* ceases to function as a reliable form of warrant. The visual record, once the bedrock of empirical verification, becomes a theater of illusion.

CSR thus redefines the question of realism for the digital age. It is no longer sufficient to ask, "Is this real?" We must ask, "What is the warrant for believing that this representation corresponds to reality?" The critical shift is from perception to method—from trusting the senses to verifying the processes that generate and validate sensory claims.

Philosophically, this marks a return to Kant's insight: knowledge does not arise directly from experience but from the disciplined synthesis of experience under the laws of reason.[6] In a world of deepfakes, the only reliable experience is the *tested* one.

3.3.6 The Collapse of the Correspondence Criterion

When AI-generated media saturate perception, the world risks entering a phase of epistemic derealization—a condition in which images proliferate faster than verification. The flood of synthetic representations overwhelms the human capacity for correspondence testing. What cannot be checked must be trusted, and trust, once eroded, yields to nihilism.

CSR warns that without an external anchor in objective reality, knowledge becomes circular. Information refers only to other information, systems to other systems. The intellectus no longer corresponds to rei but to itself. This is the very inversion that postmodernism celebrated and that CSR was built to resist. The digital simulacrum has thus fulfilled the prophecy of relativism: the map has replaced the territory.

The only defense is philosophical vigilance—the deliberate reassertion of the distinction between representation and being. Verification must evolve alongside simulation. Cryptographic watermarking, provenance tracking, and cross-modal validation are technological analogues of CSR's Critical Method. They transform skepticism into system, making truth once again a matter of method rather than perception.

3.3.7 The Algorithmic Manufacture of Reality

Beyond isolated deceptions, AI actively constructs social reality through algorithmic curation. Recommendation systems determine which news, products, and even friendships users encounter. These mechanisms subtly shape desires, fears, and beliefs, performing a kind of automated social engineering. As Foucault

---

6. Kant, *Critique of Pure Reason*.

PART ONE: THE EPISTEMIC COMMAND

argued, power operates most effectively not by coercion but by normalization—by defining what counts as knowledge, what behaviors are visible, and what voices are amplified.[7]

In this sense, algorithms have become epistemic institutions, governing the distribution of attention much as medieval scholastic authorities once governed access to scripture. They define what is thinkable by defining what is seen. The user's horizon of reality is thus algorithmically delimited—a digital echo of Plato's cave, in which the shadows are data visualizations and the fire is machine learning.

CSR insists that liberation begins with critical awareness of this structure. To apply the Scrutiny of Power—the fourth aspect of Criticality—is to unmask the invisible governance of cognition. Every recommendation engine carries implicit values; every dataset embeds a worldview. The philosophical task is to bring these to light.

3.3.8 Algorithmic Bias and the Automation of Injustice

No discussion of digital realism can ignore the problem of bias. AI systems trained on historical data inherit the prejudices of that data, amplifying them through automation.[8] Hiring algorithms that learn from discriminatory corporate histories, predictive policing systems that over-target marginalized communities, or credit models that penalize the poor—all illustrate how statistical "objectivity" can become a mask for structural injustice.

From CSR's standpoint, such systems fail the Axiological Distinction between truth and utility. They may be efficient, but they are not just; they may predict accurately within a biased dataset, but their correspondence to moral reality—the realm of fairness

---

7. Foucault, *Discipline and Punish*.
8. O'Neil, *Weapons of Math Destruction*.

CHAPTER THREE: KNOWLEDGE IN THE AGE OF AI

and dignity—is false. Knowledge divorced from ethics degenerates into control.

CSR thus extends its critique beyond metaphysics to ethics: truth is not merely an epistemic property but a moral one. The adequation of intellect to reality must include the reality of the *other*—the lived truth of human experience. Any system that suppresses or distorts this dimension, no matter how computationally elegant, fails the test of warranted knowledge.

3.3.9 The Human Cost of Epistemic Disorientation

The collapse of digital realism has psychological and social consequences. Constant exposure to contradictory or fabricated information breeds epistemic fatigue—a state of paralysis in which individuals lose confidence in the very possibility of truth. This fatigue, in turn, fuels political apathy, cynicism, and susceptibility to demagoguery. In such a climate, freedom becomes fragile, for as CSR argues, *agency depends on warranted knowledge.*

Counseling psychology, which studies the effects of cognitive dissonance and uncertainty,[9] offers a revealing parallel. Just as personal well-being requires coherence between belief and reality, social health requires coherence between shared narratives and objective truth. A society inundated with misinformation resembles a patient trapped in delusion—defensive, fragmented, unable to act coherently. The philosophical therapist's task is the same as the psychological one: to restore contact with reality.

3.3.10 Toward a Renewed Digital Realism

To restore epistemic stability in the digital age, CSR prescribes a new form of Digital Realism—a framework that reasserts the principles of correspondence and criticality within algorithmic systems. This entails several practical imperatives:

---

9. Festinger, *Theory of Cognitive Dissonance.*

PART ONE: THE EPISTEMIC COMMAND

1. Transparency as Correspondence:

   Systems must reveal the provenance and logic of their outputs. Explainability is not a technical luxury but a metaphysical necessity. What cannot be inspected cannot be believed.

2. Accountability as Coherence:

   Algorithmic decisions must integrate with coherent ethical frameworks. A model that predicts effectively but violates justice is epistemically incoherent at the moral level.

3. Human Oversight as Reason and Experience:

   Critical Rationalism demands human participation in every high-stakes decision loop. Machines can simulate inference but not understanding; human judgment must close the circle.

4. Public Literacy as Criticality:

   Citizens must cultivate philosophical literacy in the age of AI—an understanding of how information is generated, filtered, and weaponized. Without this, democratic agency erodes.

Digital Realism is therefore not a rejection of AI but its philosophical domestication. It subordinates computation to comprehension, restoring the hierarchy that CSR regards as sacred: truth above utility, reason above efficiency, reality above relevance.

3.3.11 The Philosophical Stakes

The rise of AI marks the greatest test of epistemology since the Enlightenment. Just as Descartes sought a foundation of certainty in a skeptical age, we must now seek a foundation of reality in an algorithmic one. CSR offers that foundation by reminding us that truth cannot be derived from statistics alone. Meaning arises not from pattern but from *participation*—the encounter between mind and world.

CHAPTER THREE: KNOWLEDGE IN THE AGE OF AI

To preserve that encounter is the moral duty of philosophy in the digital century. For if we lose the distinction between what is *real* and what is *reinforced*, we will have traded the splendor of truth for the glitter of computation.

3.4 CRITICALITY, POWER, AND THE ETHICS OF TRANSPARENCY

3.4.1 The Return of Critical Philosophy

Every technological revolution calls forth a new form of critique. When Gutenberg's press transformed information into a mass commodity, theology had to reinvent its authority; when the steam engine mechanized labor, political economy had to reimagine justice; and now, as algorithms mechanize thought, philosophy must reclaim criticality—the disciplined scrutiny of how knowledge is produced, validated, and distributed.

For Critical Synthetic Realism (CSR), criticality is not mere suspicion. It is an *ethical method* grounded in the duty to test every claim—scientific, political, or digital—against the twin standards of correspondence (to reality) and coherence (within reason). The aim is liberation from illusion. But in the digital age, illusion no longer comes from superstition or ignorance; it emanates from *opacity*. The problem is not that people believe in magic, but that they trust the machine.

The rise of black-box algorithms—systems so complex that even their creators cannot fully explain their internal logic[10]—marks a crisis of epistemic transparency. If a knowledge claim cannot be publicly inspected or falsified, it cannot, under CSR, qualify as warranted knowledge. The epistemic opacity of machine learning thus reintroduces an old danger under a new guise: *authority without accountability*. Where medieval societies deferred to

---

10. Lipton, "Mythos of Model Interpretability."

divine revelation, modern societies risk deferring to algorithmic revelation.

Criticality, then, becomes the essential philosophical act of the 21st century—the reassertion of human reason over computational mystique.

3.4.2 The Methodological Crisis: Falsification and the Black Box

The principle of falsification, as articulated by Karl Popper,[11] is the cornerstone of scientific and philosophical progress. Knowledge grows through the systematic elimination of error; what cannot be tested cannot be trusted. CSR adopts this principle as the engine of epistemic integrity. Yet AI systems, particularly deep neural networks, challenge falsification at its core.

Deep learning models generate outputs based on millions—or even billions—of parameters optimized through training data. Their inner workings are not rule-based but emergent. This makes them immensely powerful, but also methodologically inscrutable. When an AI system classifies a tumor as malignant, approves a loan, or predicts a criminal risk, the rationale for its decision may be mathematically encoded yet philosophically invisible.

From a CSR standpoint, this opacity nullifies the criterion of warrant. A claim whose justification cannot be examined by reason is epistemically inert—it may be accurate, but it is not *knowledge*. The distinction between *correctness* and *truth* becomes crucial here: correctness is the empirical alignment of output with outcome; truth is the justified alignment of intellect with reality. A correct answer without justification is a coincidence, not an insight.

Therefore, CSR calls for an Epistemology of Explainability: algorithms must not only perform but *account* for their performance. Their processes must be reconstructed in humanly

---

11. Popper, *Logic of Scientific Discovery*.

comprehensible terms, allowing for public testing and falsification. This is not a technical afterthought—it is the ethical heart of epistemology in the age of AI.

3.4.3 Transparency as an Epistemic Virtue

Transparency, in the CSR framework, is more than a procedural value; it is a philosophical virtue—the external manifestation of intellectual honesty. It arises from the same ethical imperative that demands truth-telling in human discourse: the willingness to expose one's reasoning to scrutiny.

For centuries, this virtue defined the progress of science. Galileo's telescopic observations, Newton's mathematical proofs, and Einstein's field equations were all falsifiable—open to replication, critique, and refinement. This culture of transparency institutionalized humility, ensuring that no claim could stand immune from evidence. But algorithmic systems, designed primarily for performance and profit, reverse this trajectory. They render reasoning proprietary, enclose logic within intellectual property rights, and privilege commercial secrecy over epistemic openness.

CSR warns that this privatization of reason constitutes a new epistemic feudalism—a digital hierarchy in which knowledge is controlled by corporate power rather than democratic deliberation. The defense of truth thus becomes inseparable from the defense of transparency. To know must remain a public act.

3.4.4 The Political Dimension: Knowledge and Power

Michel Foucault argued that knowledge is never neutral; it is always entangled with power.[12] The institutions that define truth also define who counts as sane, normal, or legitimate. CSR extends this insight into the algorithmic age: when AI systems classify, sort, and rank human beings, they perform a new kind

---

12. Foucault, *Discipline and Punish*.

of governance—epistemic governance—in which power operates through data.

An algorithm that predicts crime risk, for example, does not merely describe reality; it helps create it. By labeling certain neighborhoods as "high-risk," it attracts increased surveillance, which generates more arrests, which then confirm the system's original assumption. The feedback loop produces not knowledge but self-fulfilling prophecy—a perfect Coherence within a false Correspondence.

CSR's Critical Rationalism demands that we expose these loops and test them against independent reality. Every classification must be interrogated:

- What data shaped it?
- What worldviews does it embed?
- Whose interests does it serve?

To perform this critique is not to reject technology, but to humanize it—to restore the moral weight of epistemic responsibility.

4.4.5 Algorithmic Bias and Moral Realism

Bias in AI systems is not merely a technical flaw; it is a symptom of deeper moral confusion. When historical data reflect injustice, algorithms trained upon them will reproduce injustice with mathematical precision.[13] CSR interprets this as a violation of the Axiological Distinction—the confusion of factual regularity with moral rightness.

In a realist framework, moral truth is not reducible to statistical prevalence. The fact that discriminatory patterns exist does not make them just. The adequation of intellect to reality must include not only descriptive reality but normative reality—the reality of human dignity and equality. Therefore, CSR calls for the

---

13. O'Neil, *Weapons of Math Destruction*.

CHAPTER THREE: KNOWLEDGE IN THE AGE OF AI

integration of Moral Realism into digital epistemology: algorithms must correspond not only to what *is*, but to what *ought to be*, when the domain of application involves human lives.

This requires more than fairness metrics. It demands a philosophy of data ethics grounded in the metaphysical conviction that truth and justice are not negotiable outcomes but objective goods.

3.4.6 Situated Ethics: Context, Impact, and Responsibility

CSR's ethical dimension insists that all knowledge claims be evaluated within their situational context—a principle parallel to liberation theology's *preferential option for the poor*. Just as theology must interpret revelation through the lived realities of the oppressed, so too must AI ethics interpret data through the lens of social impact.

This perspective gives rise to Situated Epistemology: understanding that every dataset is a cultural artifact, every algorithm a political text. To claim neutrality is to conceal responsibility. Thus, CSR's moral imperative extends to the design phase of technology itself. The training data, feature selection, and model architecture are not value-free—they are acts of choice that carry moral consequences.

To act ethically within the CSR framework is to design systems whose epistemic assumptions are *explicit, examinable, and accountable*. This transforms transparency from an academic ideal into a civic duty.

3.4.7 From Control to Care: The Ethics of the Critical Mind

In counseling psychology, healing begins not with control but with awareness—the act of seeing one's patterns clearly. CSR applies this insight to the digital psyche. The first ethical task of the information age is not to dominate technology but to become *conscious* of it.

Human reason must transition from a logic of domination to a logic of care. This does not mean sentimentalism; it means responsible attention. Criticality, when practiced as care, becomes the epistemic equivalent of empathy: the commitment to understand before judging, to reveal before exploiting. In an era of automated decision-making, such an ethic is revolutionary.

CSR thus reframes the role of the philosopher, engineer, and policymaker alike. Each becomes a custodian of the light—a guardian ensuring that the illumination of knowledge does not blind but guides.

3.4.8 Institutionalizing Criticality

To operationalize these principles, societies must embed criticality into the architecture of governance, education, and technology. CSR suggests four institutional reforms:

1. Transparent Design Mandates:

    All high-impact AI systems should be subject to explainability requirements equivalent to scientific peer review. No decision affecting human welfare should be based on an uninspectable model.

2. Epistemic Impact Assessments:

    Just as environmental assessments measure ecological risk, epistemic assessments would measure the potential for misinformation, bias, or epistemic harm in algorithmic systems.

3. Ethical Literacy Education:

    Philosophy, logic, and critical reasoning should become central to digital education. The next generation must learn not only to use AI but to question it.

CHAPTER THREE: KNOWLEDGE IN THE AGE OF AI

4. Global Governance of Data Justice:
International cooperation should treat data integrity as a universal human right. Truth must not be privatized; it is a common good.

These measures translate CSR's metaphysical principles into social practice. They make truth not only thinkable but governable.

3.4.9 The Ethical Horizon: Truth as Liberation

Ultimately, the ethics of CSR converge on a single humanistic vision: truth as liberation. The purpose of critical inquiry, whether in theology, science, or AI, is to free the mind from constraint—be it dogma, bias, or technological determinism. Liberation here is not rebellion against reality but reconciliation with it. To know truly is to live freely within the order of the real.

The digital age tempts humanity with a counterfeit freedom—the illusion of infinite choice generated by algorithms that quietly dictate those choices. CSR counters this with a deeper freedom: the freedom of *discernment*, the capacity to know why we choose what we choose. In this, criticality becomes an act of self-respect, and transparency an act of love.

3.5 CONCLUSION: INFORMATION EXPANSION AND WISDOM MAINTENANCE

3.5.1 The Paradox of Abundance

We stand at the most paradoxical moment in the history of human cognition: never have we possessed so much information, and yet never have we been so unsure of what it means. Humanity has built vast digital libraries that update themselves in milliseconds, trained models that write with flawless grammar, and created networks that simulate omniscience. Yet beneath this abundance lies an epistemic famine—the slow starvation of *wisdom*.

PART ONE: THE EPISTEMIC COMMAND

Knowledge, in its true philosophical sense, has always been more than the possession of facts. It is the capacity to discern truth from appearance, essence from noise, the real from the relevant. But as Artificial Intelligence expands the production of information to planetary scale, it also compresses the time available for reflection. The human mind, evolved for depth, now struggles to survive in an ecosystem optimized for speed.

CSR identifies this as the epistemic crisis of acceleration: when the velocity of data exceeds the capacity of reason, comprehension yields to automation. The danger is not that machines will surpass us intellectually, but that we will *surrender the discipline of thinking*—outsourcing the labor of understanding to algorithms that know everything except meaning.

Thus, the defining philosophical challenge of the 21st century is not how to make AI conscious, but how to keep *human consciousness critical*.

3.5.2 CSR as the Compass of the Digital Mind

Critical Synthetic Realism (CSR) provides the necessary compass for navigating this age of artificial knowledge. It teaches that truth must always satisfy four conditions:

1. Metaphysical Realism—Knowledge must correspond to an objective reality, independent of our preferences or algorithms.
2. Epistemic Pluralism—Claims must satisfy both Coherence (internal consistency) and Correspondence (external verification).
3. Critical Rationalism—Every belief must remain open to falsification, revision, and public critique.
4. Axiological Distinction—Truth must never be reduced to utility, convenience, or engagement. Its moral worth lies in its integrity.

CHAPTER THREE: KNOWLEDGE IN THE AGE OF AI

In the AI context, these pillars translate into four imperatives:

CSR Pillar	Digital Imperative
Realism	Preserve reference to an objective world; demand empirical verification of data.
Pluralism	Balance algorithmic coherence with independent human oversight.
Critical Rationalism	Require explainability, reproducibility, and transparency of models.
Axiological Distinction	Reject engagement metrics as proxies for truth; re-center epistemic ethics.

By applying these principles, humanity can transform AI from a mirror of chaos into an instrument of clarity. CSR does not reject technology—it disciplines it. It insists that information becomes knowledge only when subjected to philosophical testing.

In this way, CSR serves as a *moral firewall*—protecting human reason from the seductions of algorithmic certainty. It is the corrective lens that restores focus in an age of optical illusions.

3.5.3 The Moral Responsibility of Knowing

Knowledge has always carried a moral dimension. To know falsely is not a neutral error—it is an act with consequences. The architects of AI now wield a power once reserved for philosophers and priests: the power to define what appears as truth. Their algorithms shape the epistemic environment within which billions form beliefs, make decisions, and imagine futures.

CSR demands that such power be exercised under the principle of epistemic responsibility—the obligation to align technological design with the moral structure of truth. It is not enough for systems to be efficient; they must also be *rightly ordered*. As with theology's ancient debates over heresy, the danger today is not ignorance but misdirected conviction—the confident repetition of coherent falsehoods.

Thus, the moral duty of the digital age is to restore humility to knowledge. Every act of prediction must carry the question: *What is my warrant?* Every claim, no matter how algorithmically sophisticated, must answer: *What justifies my truth?*

Philosophy, in this sense, becomes the conscience of technology.

3.5.4 The Future of Reason: Coevolution, Not Competition

The relationship between human and machine intelligence need not be adversarial. Properly ordered, it can be coevolutionary. CSR envisions a future in which AI expands the scope of human perception while reason preserves the standards of judgment. The goal is not to build artificial minds, but to cultivate *augmented wisdom*—a synthesis of computational capacity and philosophical discernment.

Machines can model probabilities; only humans can discern purpose. Algorithms can optimize efficiency; only humans can deliberate on justice. AI can generate information; only the reflective intellect can transform it into meaning. These asymmetries are not weaknesses—they are the foundations of our agency.

The danger lies in mistaking assistance for authority. When humanity begins to ask machines not "What do you compute?" but "What should we believe?", the abdication of reason begins. CSR therefore insists that every technological system must remain nested within human epistemic oversight. The machine may inform, but only the human may *affirm*.

This reaffirmation of human centrality is not arrogance—it is accountability. To know is to be responsible for what one believes. That responsibility cannot be delegated to code.

CHAPTER THREE: KNOWLEDGE IN THE AGE OF AI

3.5.5 Wisdom as the Moral Apex of Knowledge

The ultimate aim of all philosophy—ancient or modern, analog or digital—is wisdom. Wisdom is the ethical culmination of knowledge: the alignment of truth with goodness. It is the point where cognition becomes conscience.

The distinction between *information*, *knowledge*, and *wisdom* is therefore not semantic but structural:

Level	Nature	Criterion of Value	CSR Equivalent
Information	Data and patterns	Volume and velocity	Coherence without warrant
Knowledge	Justified true belief	Correspondence and coherence	Full synthetic warrant
Wisdom	Judged truth integrated with moral purpose	Justice and human flourishing	Axiological fulfillment

AI, for all its brilliance, operates only at the first level. It processes information. It can approximate knowledge through statistical accuracy but cannot rise to wisdom, because wisdom presupposes *ethical intentionality*. It requires awareness of value, empathy, and the ends of human life—dimensions beyond computation.

CSR thus affirms that the highest form of intelligence is not artificial but moral. To preserve wisdom amid information expansion is to preserve our humanity itself.

3.5.6 Restoring the Human Center

As we move deeper into the algorithmic century, we must resist the drift toward epistemic decentralization—the idea that truth resides nowhere because it resides everywhere. The *splendor of truth* is not in its diffusion but in its clarity. Philosophy must reclaim its ancient role as the custodian of that light.

To restore the human center in a world of digital shadows requires a renewed spiritual confidence in reason. This does not mean reviving metaphysical arrogance; it means recognizing that rational inquiry, when guided by humility, is itself an act of reverence. To seek truth is to honor reality.

Here, theology, philosophy, and psychology converge. The theologian's reverence, the philosopher's rigor, and the counselor's empathy all meet in the same pursuit: understanding the human condition truthfully. In my own intellectual journey—across theology, philosophy, computer science, business, communication, and counseling psychology—this conviction has become central: *knowledge must humanize, or it fails its purpose.*

AI expands what we can do; CSR ensures we remember *why*.

3.5.7 The Splendor of Truth in the Age of Algorithms

The title of this book—*The Splendor of Truth*—finds its full meaning here. The "splendor" is not mystical illumination but the radiant coherence of reality revealed through disciplined inquiry. It is the light that shines when intellect aligns with being. In an age dazzled by synthetic brilliance, philosophy must remind us that true light does not blind—it clarifies.

The future of knowledge depends not on machines that can speak but on humans who can still listen—to evidence, to reason, and to conscience. The task ahead is not to build better algorithms but to become better knowers.

CSR offers that path: a rational spirituality grounded in truth, a philosophy that binds knowledge to virtue, and a realism that anchors freedom in the real. It teaches that to preserve truth in a digital world is to defend the very possibility of meaning.

CHAPTER THREE: KNOWLEDGE IN THE AGE OF AI

For in the end, knowledge without truth is noise, information without justice is manipulation, and intelligence without conscience is peril.

The splendor of truth—hard-earned, self-correcting, and luminous—is humanity's only reliable light. AI may multiply our signals, but only philosophy can preserve our sight.

PART TWO: REFUTATION—CONQUERING THE FORCES OF IRRATIONALITY

CHAPTER FOUR: WITCHCRAFT AS PHILOSOPHICALLY UNJUSTIFIABLE

4.1 PHILOSOPHY'S TASK OF REFUTATION

Philosophy, as Socrates taught, is the art of living examined lives. To examine is to expose illusion—to unmask the shadows that imprison thought. Every civilization must eventually confront its own epistemic idols: myths masquerading as knowledge, narratives mistaken for explanation. Witchcraft, perhaps more than any other belief, represents this perennial struggle between mythos and logos—between the narrative mind and the rational intellect.

In every age, witchcraft reappears under new names: demons in medieval Europe, juju in West Africa, psychic energy in the New Age movement, or "generational curses" in some Pentecostal churches. Its essence is unchanged: the conviction that unseen personal agents control material outcomes. This chapter treats witchcraft not as superstition in the pejorative sense, but as a system of thought—one that satisfies human emotional needs while violating philosophical standards of truth.

PART TWO: REFUTATION

CSR approaches this belief as a case study in refutation. Refutation, in the CSR sense, is not ridicule or cultural condemnation; it is a disciplined demonstration of why a claim fails to meet the logical, empirical, and ethical tests of reality. True liberation—intellectual and social—depends on such philosophical clarity.

4.2 THE ANATOMY OF OCCULT CAUSALITY

At the heart of witchcraft is the concept of occult causality—the notion that hidden, non-physical agents (witches, spirits, curses) can directly produce physical effects. The witch becomes the unseen variable that fills explanatory gaps in misfortune. Anthropologist E. E. Evans-Pritchard observed among the Azande of Central Africa that witchcraft served as a *theory of coincidence*: termites cause a granary to collapse, but witchcraft explains *why it collapsed at that particular time on that particular person*.[1]

Such reasoning arises from a universal human desire for personal causality: to find meaning in randomness. Yet, from a philosophical standpoint, it fails both Metaphysical Realism and Causal Coherence. For CSR, every valid causal claim must satisfy two conditions:

1. Causal Adequacy—The cause must possess sufficient power to produce the effect.
2. Ontological Accessibility—The cause must exist within, or be demonstrably linked to, the same ontological domain as the effect.

Occult causality satisfies neither. Invisible agents lack empirical evidence of existence (violating Correspondence), and no verifiable mechanism links mental or spiritual malice to physical outcomes (violating Causal Closure). Witchcraft thus exemplifies a category error—it projects emotional and moral meanings into the causal fabric of the universe.

---

1. Evans-Pritchard, *Witchcraft, Oracles, and Magic*.

CHAPTER FOUR: WITCHCRAFT

4.3 THE HISTORICAL EVOLUTION OF WITCHCRAFT THINKING

4.3.1 Ancient and Medieval Roots

The witchcraft worldview originates in humanity's pre-scientific consciousness. Early cosmologies—Babylonian, Egyptian, Greek—saw nature as alive with spirits. Aristotle's *Physics* (4th century BCE) hinted at natural explanation, yet even he could not fully sever the world from teleological "final causes." Medieval thought, blending Aristotelian metaphysics with Christian theology, inherited this ambiguity.

Augustine (354–430 CE) denounced pagan magic as diabolical deception, yet accepted the existence of supernatural intermediaries. Aquinas retained this hierarchy but distinguished sharply between *miracle* (divine suspension of nature) and *magic* (human attempt to usurp it).[2] Witchcraft thus became not only epistemically suspect but morally inverted—a rebellion against divine order.

4.3.2 The Enlightenment and Skeptical Revolution

By the 17th century, the Enlightenment challenged the metaphysical infrastructure of witchcraft. Hume exposed miracles and magic alike to the test of empirical probability: no testimony, however strong, can outweigh uniform experience of natural law.[3] The Scientific Revolution's principle of causal closure—that every physical effect has a physical cause—destroyed the intellectual foundation of witchcraft even as social fear kept it alive.

In this historical light, witchcraft is not merely a primitive residue but a recurring epistemic temptation: the longing to personify uncertainty. It survives wherever anxiety exceeds explanation.

---

2. Thomas Aquinas, *Summa Theologica*.
3. Hume, *Enquiry Concerning Human Understanding*.

PART TWO: REFUTATION

4.4 THE FAILURE OF EPISTEMIC CRITERIA

4.4.1 Correspondence and Empirical Adequation

According to CSR, truth requires *adaequatio intellectus et rei*—the conformity of intellect to reality. Witchcraft claims lack any such conformity. No controlled study has verified psychic attack, spiritual poisoning, or physical transmutation by intention. Every alleged instance yields to natural explanation—disease, coincidence, social conflict, or suggestibility.

This is not arrogance of science; it is discipline of reason. As CSR teaches, to affirm a claim without evidence is not humility—it is irresponsibility. The intellectual virtue of humility lies in admitting ignorance, not sanctifying it.

4.4.2 Coherence without Correspondence

Witchcraft beliefs exhibit remarkable internal coherence. Within the cultural system, they are logically consistent: if envy causes bewitchment, and witches exist, misfortune naturally follows. But coherence without correspondence is not knowledge—it is narrative. The system explains itself perfectly while explaining nothing about the world.

CSR thus diagnoses witchcraft as a coherence-closed system—self-reinforcing but epistemically sterile. Like tautological ideologies, it survives by forbidding disproof. Any counterevidence is reinterpreted as proof of deeper conspiracy.

4.4.3 The Falsification Barrier

Following Popper,[4] CSR defines knowledge as conjecture tested by falsification. Witchcraft fails because it cannot specify conditions under which it would be false. Its epistemic structure is circular:

---

4. Popper, *Logic of Scientific Discovery*.

CHAPTER FOUR: WITCHCRAFT

- *If the accused confesses:* proof of witchcraft.
- *If the accused denies:* proof of deceit (also witchcraft).
- *If no evidence appears:* proof of invisibility (stronger witchcraft).

Such reasoning collapses under Modus Tollens: if the theory predicts evidence that fails to appear, the theory must be false. Witchcraft thus stands outside the domain of rational discourse. It is, as Kant might say, a "regulative illusion."

4.5 PSYCHOLOGICAL FUNCTIONS OF WITCHCRAFT BELIEF

While epistemically invalid, witchcraft persists because it meets deep psychological needs. From the standpoint of counseling psychology, the belief functions as both a defense mechanism and a social coping strategy.

4.5.1 Projection and the Shadow Self

Freud understood projection as the displacement of unacceptable impulses onto others.[5] Witchcraft serves precisely this function: internal envy, aggression, or guilt is externalized as malevolent others. Jung extended this insight with his concept of the shadow—the disowned aspects of the psyche that reappear in mythic form.[6] The witch is the collective shadow of the community—an image of its repressed fears, desires, and failures.

Counseling psychology recognizes such projection as a form of anxiety management. By locating evil outside oneself, one avoids confronting personal responsibility. Yet this evasion perpetuates psychic immaturity, keeping both individuals and societies trapped in paranoia.

---

5. Freud, *Totem and Taboo*.
6. Jung, *Man and His Symbols*.

PART TWO: REFUTATION

4.5.2 Control and the Psychology of Fear

Human beings have an intrinsic need for control. Uncertainty is intolerable; randomness feels like chaos. Witchcraft provides an illusion of control by supplying intentionality where none exists. If one can identify the witch, one can neutralize misfortune. Rituals, charms, or exorcisms offer comfort by symbolically restoring order.

From a clinical perspective, this is an *adaptive illusion*: it regulates anxiety but distorts cognition. True healing requires not ritual blame but existential acceptance—acknowledging that suffering, while real, is not always moralized or targeted. The refusal to accept chance fuels the persistence of magical thinking.

4.5.3 Cognitive Biases and Social Reinforcement

Cognitive psychology identifies multiple biases that sustain witchcraft belief:

- Confirmation bias: selective recall of events that confirm pre-existing beliefs.
- Post hoc reasoning: assuming causation from mere sequence.
- Availability heuristic: overestimating the frequency of vivid, memorable cases.

These biases are amplified by social reinforcement. In close-knit communities, shared narratives are rewarded with belonging, while skepticism is punished as arrogance. Thus, witchcraft belief becomes not only cognitive but communal—a system of epistemic conformity.

CHAPTER FOUR: WITCHCRAFT

4.6 THE SOCIOLOGY OF FEAR AND MORAL ORDER

4.6.1 Witchcraft as Social Explanation

In African contexts, as Mbiti[7] and Evans-Pritchard[8] noted, witchcraft functions less as individual superstition than as moral sociology. It explains why bad things happen to good people in a world where social harmony is prized. When misfortune strikes, someone must have violated the moral equilibrium. Witchcraft restores that equilibrium symbolically, even if it destroys real people.

CSR interprets this as an epistemic misplacement of justice—the confusion of moral causality with physical causality. The desire for fairness distorts the perception of nature. Instead of accepting that drought or disease can be impersonal, the community personalizes misfortune, thereby maintaining moral coherence at the cost of truth.

4.6.2 Witchcraft Accusations and the Politics of Power

Witchcraft accusations often target the powerless—women, the elderly, or outsiders—turning epistemic error into structural violence. Here, CSR intersects with liberation theology, which views truth not only as correspondence but as a weapon against oppression. False beliefs that sustain injustice become moral evils.

The witch trials of Europe and the accusations in African villages follow the same psychological law: fear weaponized by power. The philosopher's duty is to expose this dynamic, for every accusation built on epistemic falsehood becomes an act of social sin.

---

7. Mbiti, *African Religions and Philosophy*.
8. Evans-Pritchard, *Witchcraft, Oracles, and Magic*.

PART TWO: REFUTATION

4.7 THE THEOLOGICAL DISTORTION OF FAITH

4.7.1 The Shift from Providence to Paranoia

In many contemporary Christian movements, particularly Pentecostalism, the language of witchcraft has been baptized rather than abolished. "Deliverance ministries" reinterpret misfortune as demonic warfare. Poverty becomes the curse of ancestral sin; depression becomes spiritual bondage.

This theological system reverses the Gospel of liberation into a gospel of suspicion. Where Christ preached forgiveness and reasoned faith, witchcraft theology preaches fear and exorcism. The congregation becomes a courtroom of accusation; suffering is moralized instead of relieved.

4.7.2 Faith Seeking Understanding

CSR reclaims the classical notion of *fides quaerens intellectum*—faith seeking understanding.[9] Faith without reason degenerates into magical thinking; reason without faith becomes sterile. The Christian philosopher must therefore distinguish between mystery (truths beyond empirical verification but coherent with moral reason) and superstition (claims that contradict reason and exploit fear).

A mature theology accepts the transcendence of God without attributing every shadow to the devil. The presence of evil is real, but its explanation must remain morally and intellectually coherent. When religion substitutes spiritual warfare for moral responsibility, it becomes complicit in the very darkness it seeks to banish.

---

9. Anselm, *Proslogion*.

CHAPTER FOUR: WITCHCRAFT

4.8 LIBERATION THEOLOGY AND THE DEMYTHOLOGIZATION OF EVIL

Liberation theology reframes sin not as occult malice but as structural injustice. The poor are not bewitched—they are exploited. The sick are not cursed—they are underserved. Evil resides not in invisible sorcerers but in visible systems of greed and neglect.

Thus, the demythologization of witchcraft is a theological act of liberation. To shift from magic to justice is to reclaim divine truth as moral truth. As Paulo Freire argued,[10] authentic liberation begins when people recognize that their oppression is not mystical but systemic. CSR provides the epistemic method for this recognition: falsification of false causes and verification of real ones.

In this sense, philosophy and theology converge. Both demand that we confront fear with reason, illusion with love, and superstition with solidarity.

4.9 THE ETHICAL MANDATE OF TRUTH

Truth, in CSR, carries moral weight. It is not enough to know; one must act on knowledge. When false beliefs produce harm, silence becomes complicity. The Axiological Distinction forbids confusing comfort with truth. To tell people what they want to hear may soothe them, but to tell them what is true dignifies them.

4.9.1 Intellectual Virtue and Moral Courage

The philosopher and counselor share the same virtue: intellectual courage. To question witchcraft in communities where it is sacred invites hostility. Yet the refusal to question perpetuates suffering. The ethical life therefore demands the willingness to risk misunderstanding in the service of liberation.

---

10. Freire, *Pedagogy of the Oppressed*.

PART TWO: REFUTATION

Philosophy, as therapy, seeks healing through truth; counseling, as philosophy, seeks truth through healing. Both disciplines converge in the principle of *logos as therapy*—reason as the healing of fear.

4.9.2 The Duty of Deconstruction

To deconstruct witchcraft belief is not to humiliate culture but to elevate it. True respect for culture involves freeing it from self-defeating illusions. Every civilization has passed through this stage: Greece left behind Homeric myth for philosophy; Europe left behind alchemy for science. Africa, too, must complete its intellectual decolonization—not by rejecting spirituality but by aligning it with truth.

4.10 REFUTATION AS HEALING: THE THERAPEUTIC FUNCTION OF PHILOSOPHY

Refutation is not destruction but purification. It removes error so that truth can breathe. In counseling psychology, catharsis (emotional release) is healing through truth-telling. In philosophy, refutation is cognitive catharsis—the release of the mind from error through evidence.

Thus, the rejection of witchcraft is not arrogance but compassion. It releases individuals from fear and communities from cycles of accusation. It restores causality to nature and morality to conscience. To refute is to heal.

4.11 CONCLUSION: THE TRIUMPH OF REASON

Under *Critical Synthetic Realism*, witchcraft collapses as a system of knowledge but remains a mirror of humanity's longing for meaning. The task of philosophy is not to mock this longing but to redirect it—from fear to understanding, from superstition to science, from accusation to empathy.

CHAPTER FOUR: WITCHCRAFT

Witchcraft fails CSR's four pillars:

- It violates Metaphysical Realism by positing non-empirical entities as physical causes.
- It fails Epistemic Pluralism, relying solely on coherence without correspondence.
- It rejects Critical Rationalism by refusing falsification.
- It breaches Axiological Integrity by producing harm in the guise of moral order.

Therefore, it cannot stand as knowledge. It is, in essence, *belief without warrant*—a relic of pre-critical thought that enslaves rather than enlightens.

The liberation from witchcraft belief is thus not merely intellectual but spiritual. It affirms humanity's capacity for truth and restores faith in the intelligibility of creation. To think critically is not to lose the sacred; it is to sanctify the real.

As Aquinas wrote, *"All truth, by whomsoever spoken, comes from the Holy Spirit."*[11] To abandon falsehood, then, is an act of worship. The defeat of witchcraft is not the death of wonder but the birth of wisdom—the dawn of the splendor of truth in the emancipated mind.

---

11. Thomas Aquinas, *Summa Theologica* II-II, Q. 172, Art. 6, arg. 1 (1952 ed.).

CHAPTER FIVE: EPISTEMIC FRACTURE AND THE CAUSE OF STAGNATION— THE CURE FOR UNDERDEVELOPMENT

The project of *The Splendor of Truth* is a demand for Global Agency—a call for humanity, and Africa in particular, to reclaim its destiny through verifiable, warranted knowledge. This chapter addresses a historical paradox: how did the cradle of human civilization—the continent that pioneered mathematics, architecture, and governance—become the epicenter of global underdevelopment? While slavery and colonialism wrought immense destruction, this chapter argues that these were *symptoms*, not causes. The deeper cause was an Epistemic Fracture: a centuries-long retreat from the critical, self-correcting method that sustained Africa's early brilliance.

Using the framework of *Critical Synthetic Realism (CSR)*, the chapter identifies this fracture as the moment when inquiry gave way to obedience, when knowledge was deified and therefore immobilized. It then examines the epistemic roots of corruption, the persistence of magical thinking, and the collapse of civic rationality.

CHAPTER FIVE: EPISTEMIC FRACTURE AND STAGNATION

Finally, it prescribes a cure grounded in the institutionalization of *Critical Thinking*, the enforcement of the *Integrity Rule*, and the creation of epistemically accountable governance. The path to development, it concludes, is not merely economic—it is philosophical: a moral commitment to truth as the foundation of freedom.

5.1 THE CRADLE, THE ZENITH, AND THE PARADOX OF VULNERABILITY

5.1.1 The Epistemic Ecology of Early African Civilization

Long before Greece dreamed of democracy or Europe discovered geometry, African civilizations had already institutionalized systems of *applied realism*: the conviction that the world could be understood, predicted, and ordered through rational inquiry and empirical verification. Ancient Egypt's concept of *Ma'at*—truth, balance, and order—was not merely a moral code but an epistemic one: a commitment to the harmony between thought and reality.

In sub-Saharan Africa, proto-scientific systems flourished in agriculture, metallurgy, and astronomy. Dogon cosmology contained accurate accounts of celestial motion long before telescopic confirmation. The Bantu concept of ubuntu, often translated as "I am because we are," implicitly encoded an *epistemic communalism*—knowledge as a cooperative endeavor tested through social experience rather than individual revelation.

CSR interprets these traditions as early forms of Synthetic Realism: knowledge produced through the synthesis of experience, reason, and moral order. These civilizations functioned as open epistemic systems—dynamic, curious, and empirically grounded.

PART TWO: REFUTATION

5.1.2 The Age of Epistemic Leadership

The empirical precision of Ancient Kemet was not an accident of genius but the result of institutionalized experimentation. The pyramids were not built by mystics but by mathematicians, engineers, and bureaucrats whose every calculation was tested against the resistance of stone and gravity.[1] The Nile flood cycles were not explained by divine caprice but by astronomical observation, resulting in the world's first solar calendar.[2]

The Kingdom of Kush, through its metallurgical revolution, exemplified technological empiricism. Iron smelting at Meroë was achieved through generations of iterative improvement—trial, error, and correction—the hallmarks of CSR's Critical Rationalism.

Meanwhile, Timbuktu, Gao, and Djenné in medieval Mali and Songhai epitomized *warranted testimony*: scholars debated jurisprudence, astronomy, and metaphysics using documented evidence and logical correspondence.[3] Knowledge was treated as a public trust—a civic good subject to verification.

This was Africa's Epistemic Zenith—a world in which progress was inseparable from the moral obligation to know truly.

5.1.3 The Paradox of Vulnerability

If Africa's early civilizations were so epistemically advanced, how did they become vulnerable to external domination? The answer, CSR contends, lies in the withdrawal of the Critical Method. When societies declare their achievements sacred, they unintentionally halt progress. By the 16th century, the dynamism of inquiry had calcified into reverence. Intellectual humility—the willingness to be wrong—was replaced by epistemic pride.

1. Aswân et al., *Geology and Archaeology*.
2. Diop, *African Origin of Civilization*.
3. Hiskett, *Development of Islam*.

CHAPTER FIVE: EPISTEMIC FRACTURE AND STAGNATION

Europe, through the Scientific Revolution, institutionalized falsifiability.[4] Africa, by contrast, sanctified coherence without correspondence—valuing harmony over critique. The result was epistemic deceleration: technological and administrative systems ceased to evolve, and the ability to adapt to external pressures vanished.

The Paradox of Vulnerability emerges here: the very reverence for tradition that once preserved social cohesion became the anchor that prevented adaptation.

5.2 THE EPISTEMIC FRACTURE—FROM DYNAMISM TO DOGMA

5.2.1 The Deification of Achievement

Every civilization risks becoming the prisoner of its own success. The Epistemic Fracture occurs when societies mistake *perfected outcomes* for *completed knowledge*. What begins as warranted discovery ends as dogma. The stages of this transmutation follow a recognizable pattern:

1. Warranted Knowledge: Knowledge grounded in empirical success and rational coherence.
2. Sacralization: Success attributed to divine revelation or ancestral perfection.
3. Protection: Challenge to established knowledge becomes taboo.
4. Decay: The prohibition of error leads to the death of innovation.

The death of falsifiability is the death of progress. When innovation becomes blasphemy, decline is inevitable.

---

4. Popper, *Logic of Scientific Discovery*.

PART TWO: REFUTATION

5.2.2 The Psychology of Dogma

CSR identifies this stage as a psychological paralysis of the intellect. Dogma is not simply wrong knowledge—it is knowledge immune to correction. The human mind, when conditioned for obedience, develops epistemic fear—a reflexive anxiety toward contradiction or novelty.

This fear manifests in education systems that reward memorization over reasoning, in politics that prize loyalty over truth, and in religions that confuse reverence with silence. The psychology of dogma replaces curiosity with conformity. Inquiry becomes rebellion; doubt becomes sin.

From a counseling psychology perspective, this constitutes collective cognitive rigidity—a cultural form of obsessive-compulsive orderliness designed to preserve social control at the cost of intellectual vitality. The result is institutional sclerosis—an inability to adapt even when survival demands it.

5.2.3 Gerontocracy and the Death of Debate

In many African societies, gerontocracy became the epistemic regime: truth was determined not by correspondence but by age. Ekeh notes that colonial governance later reinforced this model by empowering compliant elders over critical youth, institutionalizing obedience as administrative virtue.[5]

The loss of error-correction mechanisms—once central to African craft guilds and scholarly disputations—meant that innovation became socially dangerous. The young could not refute the old without being branded arrogant. The result was a frozen epistemology: coherent, stable, but unresponsive.

---

5. Ekeh, "Colonialism."

CHAPTER FIVE: EPISTEMIC FRACTURE AND STAGNATION

5.2.4 The Four Failures of the Synthetic Loop

CSR posits that the Synthetic Loop—Reason, Experience, Coherence, Testimony—is the engine of knowledge. When any element is corrupted, the loop collapses:

CSR Element	Corruption	Result
Reason	Becomes rationalization	Dogmatic justification of failure
Experience	Dismissed as irrelevant	Disconnection from reality
Coherence	Overvalued against reality	Ideological rigidity
Testimony	Becomes propaganda	Collapse of public trust

This systemic failure explains why once-innovative civilizations could no longer respond to external shocks. Their epistemic immune system—the ability to self-correct—had died.

5.3 EPISTEMIC UNDERDEVELOPMENT—THE ROOT OF MATERIAL POVERTY

5.3.1 Corruption as Epistemic Disease

Corruption is not simply theft—it is ontological deceit: the substitution of appearance for reality. It thrives where unwarranted testimony replaces evidence. In CSR terms, corruption is the systemic rejection of Correspondence.

When officials claim roads exist that do not, when budgets are declared "spent" on invisible projects, the state enters an epistemic crisis: reality no longer matters. The collapse of the Integrity Rule—the principle that all public statements must be warranted—produces political nihilism: nothing is believed because nothing corresponds to fact.

PART TWO: REFUTATION

This explains why conventional anti-corruption campaigns often fail: they attack symptoms, not the underlying epistemology. A society that rewards lies as loyalty cannot sustain truth as virtue.

5.3.2 The Epistemic Economy

Economic innovation depends on epistemic infrastructure—education, data transparency, and meritocracy. Societies that confuse opinion with evidence cannot sustain complex economies. The failure of African industrialization is thus not merely financial but cognitive: innovation requires falsifiable experimentation, yet many institutions reward conformity.

CSR introduces the concept of an Epistemic Economy—a system where ideas are tested, failures are tolerated, and correction is celebrated. Without this, even abundant resources yield poverty, because human capital remains epistemically trapped.

5.3.3 The Paralysis of Occult Causality

As Chapter 4 demonstrated, Occult Causality replaces empirical inquiry with spiritual blame. This epistemic misattribution wastes resources, misguides policy, and destroys morale. CSR defines this as the "inversion of inquiry"—the mind turned outward toward illusion rather than inward toward correction.

In public administration, this leads to policy paralysis: if drought is caused by angry ancestors, irrigation engineers are irrelevant; if poverty is caused by curses, economists are impotent. The problem is not lack of belief but belief in the wrong dimension.

CHAPTER FIVE: EPISTEMIC FRACTURE AND STAGNATION

5.3.4 Internal Fragmentation and the Logic of Weakness

Rodney showed that internal collaboration with colonial powers was not simply moral weakness but epistemic confusion—an inability to distinguish truth from expediency.[6] The betrayal of collective interest for individual patronage is an epistemic failure: truth subordinated to tribe.

CSR's analysis suggests that slavery and colonialism succeeded not because of European genius alone, but because of African epistemic fragmentation—the inability to form a shared, evidence-based worldview capable of unified resistance. The loss of the Integrity Rule meant the loss of solidarity.

5.4 THE CURE—CRITICAL THINKING, INTEGRITY, AND MORAL RENAISSANCE

5.4.1 Reclaiming the Critical Mind

The cure begins with Critical Thinking—the civic practice of asking, "What is the warrant?" Every citizen must be trained in methodological skepticism: to demand evidence for every claim, whether from priest, politician, or elder.

This is not rebellion; it is responsibility. The uncritical mind is the tyrant's best ally. The critical mind is the only guarantee of freedom.

5.4.2 Reconstructing Education

Education must evolve from rote preservation to methodological inquiry. Following Dewey,[7] learning should be an experiment in thinking, not obedience. CSR adds that schools must explicitly

---

6. Rodney, *How Europe Underdeveloped Africa*.
7. Dewey, *Democracy and Education*.

teach the *Synthetic Loop* as a civic method: every statement must be judged by its Reason, Experience, Coherence, and Testimony.

Curricula should privilege inquiry over memory, hypothesis over recitation, and truth-seeking over authority. The classroom must become a *laboratory of democracy*—the first arena where children learn that disagreement, when justified, is noble.

5.4.3 Institutionalizing the Integrity Rule

The Integrity Rule must become constitutional principle: no public claim without public warrant. This transforms government into a *verifiable enterprise*. Policies must be designed as falsifiable hypotheses with measurable outcomes, not as rhetorical promises.

CSR proposes a Public Falsifiability Framework:

1. Hypothesis Formulation: Every public project must specify the expected outcomes and timeframe.
2. Periodic Verification: Independent agencies audit progress using empirical evidence.
3. Public Correction: Failure is disclosed and corrected, not hidden.

This model ensures that truth, not loyalty, becomes the metric of success.

5.4.4 Meritocracy and Epistemic Justice

Meritocracy is not elitism—it is epistemic justice: the principle that public office belongs to those whose claims to competence are *warranted*. Age, tribe, and patronage are unwarranted testimony. Competence, verifiable through performance and education, is warranted.

CHAPTER FIVE: EPISTEMIC FRACTURE AND STAGNATION

CSR argues that democracy without epistemic integrity degenerates into populism: the rule of the loudest, not the wisest. Governance must therefore be reconstructed around *evidence-based merit*.

5.4.5 Cultural Renaissance and the Media of Truth

To reverse epistemic decay, societies must reform not only schools and parliaments but also their cultural instruments—media, art, and religion. The storyteller, filmmaker, and journalist become the new custodians of truth.

Public broadcasting should model *verifiable journalism*—investigative reporting that aligns with CSR's Correspondence Criterion. Universities must reclaim their public vocation as "truth laboratories." Religious institutions must rediscover the prophetic courage to say, *Thus says reason*, as well as *Thus says the Lord*.

The moral renaissance of a civilization begins when it re-honors truth as sacred.

5.4.6 A CSR Manifesto for Development

1. Reality is the First Resource: Without correspondence, no claim has value.
2. Inquiry is Sacred: Questioning authority is not rebellion but reverence for truth.
3. Error is Progress: A society that cannot be wrong cannot grow.
4. Integrity is Infrastructure: Honest data and transparent governance are the true engines of development.
5. Truth is Freedom: No nation is poor that can tell itself the truth.

PART TWO: REFUTATION

5.5 CONCLUSION: RECLAIMING GLOBAL AGENCY

The tragedy of African underdevelopment is not that it began late, but that it ceased to think freely. The continent that once built pyramids of precision became trapped in temples of dogma. Slavery and colonialism exploited this intellectual vulnerability, but they did not create it.

The cure, therefore, is not foreign aid or external validation. It is the resurrection of the critical mind—the return of courage to question, to test, to fail, and to begin again. CSR offers the blueprint: a moral-epistemic revolution grounded in realism, coherence, and integrity.

To restore Africa's agency is to restore its faith in reason. When truth becomes the organizing principle of governance, when falsifiability replaces flattery, and when citizens are free to think critically without fear, Africa will not merely recover—it will lead.

For in the end, development is not the accumulation of wealth but the cultivation of wisdom. And wisdom, as the splendor of truth, is the highest form of freedom.

CHAPTER SIX: REFUTATION OF DESTINY—THE FALLACY OF FATALISM

6.1 INTRODUCTION: THE UNIVERSAL ALLURE OF DESTINY

From the dawn of human civilization, the idea of destiny has exercised a powerful hold on the collective imagination. Every culture has articulated, in mythic or philosophical form, some version of the belief that life unfolds according to a preordained script: the Greek *Moira* spinning the thread of fate, the Roman *Fatum* determining each citizen's fortune, the Hindu law of *karma*, the Chinese concept of *ming*, the Islamic doctrine of *qadar*, and the Christian notion of predestination. Even modern secular thought has produced its own variants—scientific determinism, genetic fatalism, and algorithmic prediction—all claiming that human behavior and outcomes are fixed by forces beyond personal control.

This widespread conviction arises from a deep existential anxiety. Confronted by uncertainty, loss, and death, human beings have sought psychological comfort in the idea that events are part of a divine or cosmic plan. If tragedy has meaning, then suffering becomes tolerable; if success is written in the stars, then effort seems

PART TWO: REFUTATION

less daunting. Destiny, in this sense, has often served as a metaphysical anesthetic against chaos. Yet its cost has been immense. By projecting causality outward—onto gods, ancestors, or systems—fatalism diminishes the scope of human agency, undermines moral responsibility, and obstructs intellectual progress.

The project of *The Splendor of Truth* stands in deliberate opposition to this tendency. Critical Synthetic Realism (CSR), the epistemological framework developed in earlier chapters, defines truth as the warranted correspondence between intellect and reality, and insists that human knowledge grows through falsification and the disciplined correction of error.[1] Fatalism, by contrast, is the abdication of falsification: a closed epistemic system that interprets every event as both inevitable and untestable. To challenge fatalism is therefore to defend not only freedom but truth itself.

This chapter argues that fatalism—whether expressed in theological dogma, scientific determinism, or cultural superstition—is the most seductive and destructive of all epistemic errors. It masquerades as humility ("it is beyond me") but in reality conceals intellectual laziness and moral evasion. Using the CSR framework, we will expose fatalism as a violation of all four philosophical pillars: it denies *Realism* by replacing conditional causation with metaphysical necessity; it rejects *Synthesis* by refusing the corrective interplay of reason and experience; it undermines *Criticality* by making all hypotheses unfalsifiable; and it corrupts *Axiological Integrity* by using the illusion of inevitability to justify injustice.

Our task, therefore, is both philosophical and ethical: to restore the idea of freedom as an epistemic achievement—the fruit of warranted knowledge and the disciplined humility to act within the real.

---

1. Popper, *Logic of Scientific Discovery.*

CHAPTER SIX: REFUTATION OF DESTINY

6.2 THE HISTORICAL LOGIC OF FATALISM

6.2.1 Ancient Roots: From the Fates to the Logos

The classical world offered fatalism its first systematic expressions. In Greek mythology, even Zeus was subject to the decrees of the *Moirai*, three goddesses who determined the lifespan of every mortal. The tragic dramas of Sophocles and Aeschylus revolved around the paradox of human striving within unalterable destiny. Oedipus, despite every attempt to evade prophecy, fulfills it by the very actions meant to resist it. This ancient motif—that the effort to escape fate only ensures its realization—established the psychological grammar of fatalism: the illusion of agency within a closed system.

Philosophical schools transformed mythic fatalism into metaphysical doctrine. The Stoics conceived the universe as a rationally ordered whole governed by the *logos*, a divine reason that determines all events according to necessity. Human wisdom, for the Stoics, consisted not in altering outcomes but in aligning the will with the inevitable. As Epictetus declared, "Do not seek for things to happen as you wish, but wish for things to happen as they do happen, and your life will go smoothly."[2] This moral resignation, though serene, erases the creative tension between knowledge and freedom that fuels progress.

Aristotle, however, sowed the seeds of resistance. In *De Interpretatione* (9), he argued that future-tense propositions—such as "there will be a sea battle tomorrow"—are neither true nor false until the event occurs. This insight, later known as the doctrine of *future contingents*, introduced logical space for genuine novelty. The future, Aristotle suggested, is *open* because not all causes are actualized; some remain potential until human choice intervenes.

---

2. Epictetus, *Enchiridion* 8, in Epictetus, *Art of Living*, 46.

PART TWO: REFUTATION

6.2.2 Eastern Determinisms and the Search for Harmony

In the East, destiny took subtler forms. Hindu cosmology articulated the law of *karma*, a moral causality linking actions across lifetimes. Properly understood, karma is not fatalism but conditional justice: one reaps what one sows. Yet popular interpretations often reduced it to metaphysical determinism—social hierarchies and misfortunes justified as the inescapable results of prior existence. The Buddhist doctrine of dependent origination sought to dissolve such rigidity by emphasizing the interdependent, transient nature of all phenomena, but the karmic logic persisted in cultural attitudes of resignation.[3]

Chinese thought offers a similar tension. The Confucian emphasis on harmony (*he*) and filial piety sometimes evolved into submission to established order, while Taoism's principle of *wu wei* ("nonaction") was misread as passivity. Yet both traditions, at their best, aimed not to abolish agency but to align it with the rhythms of nature—an early intuition of what CSR calls *conditional causation*: the world as structured but not closed.

6.2.3 Theological Fatalism in Abrahamic Traditions

Within the Abrahamic faiths, the problem of destiny became a central theological controversy. In Christianity, Augustine's defense of divine foreknowledge against Pelagius's advocacy of free will set the pattern for centuries of debate. Calvin later radicalized the doctrine of predestination, asserting that salvation or damnation was decreed "before the foundation of the world." Islam confronted a parallel division between the *Jabriyyah*, who denied human freedom in favor of divine compulsion, and the *Qadariyyah*, who affirmed human responsibility. Judaism, though less systematically fatalistic, wrestled with the prophetic tension between divine sovereignty and moral choice.

3. Rahula, *What the Buddha Taught*.

CHAPTER SIX: REFUTATION OF DESTINY

In each case, fatalism emerged as a pious overreach of metaphysics: an attempt to preserve divine omnipotence by erasing human autonomy. Yet the ethical consequence was disastrous. If every act is willed by God, then evil becomes unintelligible and justice incoherent. To punish sin in a predestined world is to condemn puppets for obeying their strings.

6.2.4 Modern Determinisms: From Mechanism to Algorithm

The Enlightenment's scientific revolution, while liberating reason from theology, reintroduced fatalism in mechanical form. Newton's universe operated like a clockwork mechanism governed by immutable laws. Laplace famously imagined a demon who, knowing the position and velocity of every particle, could predict the entire future. Determinism thus migrated from divine decree to physical necessity.

Twentieth-century physics fractured this illusion. Quantum indeterminacy and chaos theory revealed unpredictability at both micro and macro scales. Yet a new determinism arose from neuroscience and data science. If the mind is a biochemical machine, and if algorithms can predict behavior from data, then freedom again appears illusory. In the digital age, *algorithmic fatalism*—the belief that our preferences, politics, and futures are statistically predetermined—threatens to become the new cosmology of inevitability.[4]

6.2.5 The Function of Fatalism: Psychological Refuge and Political Tool

Across these traditions, fatalism performs two enduring functions. Psychologically, it provides meaning in the face of uncertainty. When misfortune strikes, it is comforting to believe that "everything happens for a reason." This cognitive closure relieves anxiety

---

4. O'Neil, *Weapons of Math Destruction*.

PART TWO: REFUTATION

but also discourages problem-solving. Sociologically, fatalism serves as a tool of power. Rulers, priests, and modern technocrats alike have discovered that populations resigned to fate rarely rebel. From the divine right of kings to economic determinism ("the market decides"), fatalism legitimates inequality by naturalizing it.

Thus, fatalism is not simply a metaphysical error; it is a political technology and a psychological defense. It replaces the dynamic tension between knowledge and freedom with the narcotic of inevitability. CSR identifies this as an epistemic pathology: the refusal to test, revise, and act upon conditional causation. To refute fatalism is therefore to restore the *Synthetic Loop*—the continual interplay of reason, experience, and critical correction that sustains both science and moral life.

6.3 THE CSR REFUTATION OF DESTINY

Fatalism, whether expressed as divine decree, cosmic necessity, or algorithmic determinism, fails every test established by Critical Synthetic Realism (CSR). It collapses under the weight of its own epistemic contradictions. Where CSR seeks warranted knowledge through correspondence, coherence, experience, and testimony, fatalism rests on unwarranted assertion. Where CSR demands falsifiability, fatalism sanctifies opacity. Where CSR promotes epistemic humility—the acceptance that our knowledge is partial but corrigible—fatalism disguises intellectual surrender as metaphysical certainty.

To understand why destiny, as a metaphysical thesis, is untenable, we must examine it against CSR's four pillars: *Metaphysical Realism*, *Epistemic Pluralism*, *Critical Rationalism*, and *Axiological Integrity*.

CHAPTER SIX: REFUTATION OF DESTINY

6.3.1 Metaphysical Realism: The World Is Law-Governed but Open

CSR begins with *Metaphysical Realism*: the conviction that reality exists independently of human perception or will, structured by consistent causal relations. However, these causal relations are not the same as deterministic chains that eliminate novelty or freedom. Reality is ordered, but its order is *conditional*, not *necessary*. In other words, the world operates according to causal laws, yet those laws admit an infinity of possible configurations depending on antecedent conditions and human intervention.[5]

Fatalism confuses *lawfulness* with *necessity*. It assumes that because physical or moral laws exist, the outcomes they govern must be fixed and unalterable. This is a categorical error. The law of gravity ensures that objects fall when unsupported, but it does not dictate whether a person will build a bridge, invent a parachute, or climb a mountain. Lawfulness establishes constraints, not outcomes. The real world is structured, not scripted.

Modern science reinforces this realist yet non-deterministic view. Quantum physics reveals probabilities, not certainties. Chaos theory shows that minuscule variations in initial conditions can produce radically different results. Evolutionary biology demonstrates that complexity arises through contingent adaptation, not preordained design. Even within neuroscience, neuroplasticity refutes the notion that the brain is a static mechanism bound by genetic predestination.[6]

To claim that "everything is meant to be" is therefore a metaphysical overreach—a violation of the empirical evidence that the universe is lawful but open, governed but indeterminate. Under CSR, freedom is not the suspension of causality but participation within it. Human beings are *causal co-agents*—participants in a structured but unfinished cosmos.

   5. Popper, *Logic of Scientific Discovery*.
   6. Doidge, *Brain That Changes Itself*.

PART TWO: REFUTATION

6.3.2 Epistemic Pluralism: Correspondence and Coherence as the Tests of Truth

The second pillar of CSR, *Epistemic Pluralism,* holds that truth is established through two convergent tests: *Correspondence* to external reality and *Coherence* within the network of established knowledge. Fatalism fails both.

Failure of Correspondence

For a claim to be true under CSR, it must correspond to observable reality. Fatalistic claims, however, are non-empirical by design. Statements like "It was meant to be" or "This was destined" are unfalsifiable. No conceivable observation could verify or refute them. They refer not to testable events but to metaphysical intentions beyond access. When confronted with counterevidence, fatalism simply absorbs it: success confirms destiny, failure demonstrates that destiny decreed failure. This circularity severs the link between belief and evidence, rendering the system epistemically sterile.

Failure of Coherence

Fatalism also collapses on the coherence test. It contradicts other well-established truths about causation, agency, and probability. To claim that outcomes are predetermined negates the demonstrable efficacy of intervention. Medicine works because actions alter outcomes; education transforms futures because human effort changes conditions. The coherence of the empirical record demands the recognition that actions produce differences. Fatalism must either deny this or retreat into metaphor, reducing "destiny" to poetic shorthand for probability—a move that abandons its metaphysical claim altogether.

CSR, by contrast, treats causation as conditional and interactive. Each event arises from a complex web of antecedents—biological, social, and volitional. The universe is thus coherent without

CHAPTER SIX: REFUTATION OF DESTINY

being closed, structured without being scripted. This view preserves the intelligibility of reality while sustaining the moral dignity of freedom.

6.3.3 Critical Rationalism: The Demand for Falsifiability

Karl Popper's principle of falsifiability remains the foundation of CSR's third pillar: *Critical Rationalism*. Knowledge progresses not through the accumulation of certainties but through the systematic elimination of errors.[7] A claim that cannot be falsified cannot be improved; it therefore belongs to the realm of belief, not knowledge.

Fatalism is, by nature, unfalsifiable. Every possible observation can be reinterpreted as confirmation of destiny. If an individual prospers, destiny favored them; if they fail, destiny ordained their downfall. The hypothesis survives every test because it allows no test. As such, it fails the central criterion of rational inquiry.

CSR exposes this circularity as the epistemic signature of authoritarian systems—religious or political—that elevate doctrine over data. When a system declares that no conceivable evidence could disprove its central claim, it transforms itself from an engine of truth into a fortress of self-justification. In that sense, fatalism is not only a metaphysical error but a moral one: it substitutes intellectual comfort for intellectual courage.

Critical Rationalism demands the opposite attitude. It invites contradiction, uncertainty, and revision. It insists that the dignity of the mind lies in its ability to correct itself. To live critically is to inhabit the open horizon of fallibility, where truth advances through the disciplined art of being wrong.

---

7. Popper, *Logic of Scientific Discovery*.

6.3.4 Axiological Integrity: The Ethics of Truth and Freedom

The fourth pillar of CSR, *Axiological Integrity*, affirms that truth and morality are inseparable. The pursuit of warranted knowledge is not merely an intellectual duty but a moral one, because all human flourishing depends on correspondence between belief and reality. To act on falsehood is to court harm; to perpetuate it knowingly is to commit injustice.

Fatalism violates this integrity by using inevitability to excuse irresponsibility. The claim "it was destined" functions as moral anesthesia. It absolves individuals and institutions from accountability. When injustice is interpreted as fate, oppressors and victims alike are relieved of ethical burden: the tyrant's cruelty becomes destiny's decree, and the victim's suffering becomes destiny's lesson. Both are lies, and both destroy the moral architecture of society.

CSR reasserts that moral responsibility presupposes epistemic openness. A person can only be responsible for actions that are genuinely possible to alter. Thus, any system—religious, political, or scientific—that denies the meaningfulness of choice undermines the very notion of ethics. As Amartya Sen observes, freedom is both the means and the end of development.[8] Without agency, moral growth collapses into superstition.

The ethical task, then, is to preserve *epistemic accountability*—to ensure that every moral claim corresponds to inspectable causes and verifiable consequences. Destiny, as a doctrine, eliminates this link. It transforms the causal into the mystical, the correctable into the inevitable. Under CSR, such a worldview is not only irrational but immoral.

---

8. Sen, *Development as Freedom*.

CHAPTER SIX: REFUTATION OF DESTINY

6.3.5 Conditional Causation and the Logic of Freedom

CSR proposes *Conditional Causation* as the philosophical alternative to both metaphysical fatalism and chaotic indeterminism. Conditional causation holds that outcomes are produced when specific conditions converge, and those conditions can be identified, altered, or prevented through rational inquiry. Freedom, therefore, is not the negation of causality but the mastery of its conditions.

For example, disease emerges from a chain of causes—pathogens, immune response, environmental exposure—but human knowledge can modify those conditions through vaccination, sanitation, and behavioral change. Poverty arises from economic structures, education, governance, and resource distribution; change those conditions, and outcomes change. This is freedom as *epistemic competence*: the ability to discern, test, and manipulate conditions to achieve desired ends.

Fatalism collapses this logic by denying conditionality. It mistakes the recognition of causality for its closure. In doing so, it erases the very space where agency operates—the interval between cause and effect that invites intervention. To recover freedom, humanity must reclaim this interval as sacred: the moral and intellectual space of inquiry.

6.3.6 The Epistemic Consequences of Destiny

The belief in destiny produces specific epistemic distortions that CSR can diagnose systematically:

PART TWO: REFUTATION

CSR Criterion	Epistemic Function	Fatalistic Distortion	Consequence
Realism	Correspondence between claim and reality	Reality interpreted through unverifiable metaphysical intentions	Replacement of empirical evidence with revelation
Synthesis	Integration of reason, experience, coherence, testimony	Suppression of contradiction; closure of inquiry	Dogmatism and intellectual stagnation
Criticality	Continuous falsification and self-correction	Claims rendered unfalsifiable	Cognitive immobility; moral passivity
Integrity	Ethical obligation to truth and accountability	Justification of injustice as destiny	Moral nihilism disguised as piety

These distortions explain why fatalistic societies, regardless of religion or region, tend to exhibit similar pathologies: resistance to innovation, tolerance for corruption, and moral complacency in the face of suffering. Where people believe that outcomes are unchangeable, experimentation ceases; where experimentation ceases, learning stops; where learning stops, decay begins.

6.3.7 Fatalism and the Death of the Future

At its core, fatalism annihilates the concept of the future. In CSR's ontology, the future is not a prewritten chapter but a field of potentialities, each actualized through interaction between knowledge and will. The fatalist, by contrast, converts the future into a completed past—a closed script awaiting enactment. This inversion drains existence of novelty and responsibility alike. To believe that one's path is fixed is to cease writing and begin reciting.

Philosophically, the death of the future is also the death of hope. Hope is not naive optimism; it is the rational expectation that new knowledge can produce new outcomes. Without the possibility of change, there is no reason to inquire, no purpose in reform, and no moral justification for action. The greatest achievement of modern science, democracy, and human rights has been to institutionalize this hope—the conviction that reality, though structured, can be transformed through reason.

CSR insists that hope is the epistemic correlate of realism. To acknowledge the world as law-governed but open is to affirm both the necessity of knowledge and the possibility of progress. The splendor of truth lies precisely in this paradox: the world resists us, yet responds to us. Fatalism erases that dialogue, leaving only silence.

6.4 THE PSYCHOLOGY OF FATALISM AND THE MYTH OF THE GENERATIONAL CURSE

6.4.1 Fatalism as a Psychological Condition

While fatalism can be articulated in theological or philosophical language, its most enduring roots are psychological. Beneath the intellectual formulations of destiny lies a universal emotional need: the craving for certainty in an unpredictable world. When individuals confront chaos—disease, poverty, natural disaster, loss—they instinctively seek patterns and meaning. The mind, intolerant of randomness, invents causes when none are apparent.[9] Fatalism is one of these inventions: an adaptive narrative that transforms anxiety into acceptance.

At a superficial level, this can have therapeutic value. The belief that "everything happens for a reason" softens grief, mitigates guilt, and provides moral coherence in tragedy. However, when generalized into a worldview, it produces *learned helplessness*—a psychological state in which individuals cease to act because they perceive no link between effort and outcome.[10]

---

9. Kahneman, *Thinking, Fast and Slow*.
10. Seligman, *Helplessness*.

PART TWO: REFUTATION

In societies dominated by fatalistic narratives, this helplessness becomes collective. Citizens stop holding leaders accountable ("God will punish them"), cease investing in innovation ("If it's meant to be, it will be"), and resign themselves to cycles of failure. Fatalism thus becomes a self-fulfilling prophecy: by believing outcomes are fixed, people ensure that they are.

From the standpoint of Critical Synthetic Realism (CSR), this is the precise moment where the *Synthetic Loop*—the dynamic interaction of reason, experience, coherence, and testimony—collapses. The fatalistic psyche breaks the causal link between knowledge and transformation. Experience no longer refines belief; it merely reinforces resignation. Reason no longer questions; it rationalizes. Testimony no longer reports; it repeats. The society or individual trapped in this cycle lives in cognitive stasis.

6.4.2 The Generational Curse: Theologized Fatalism

A particularly virulent form of fatalism appears in certain religious cultures through the doctrine of the generational curse—the belief that moral or material misfortune is transmitted across family lines by divine decree. Among fundamentalist communities in Africa, Latin America, and parts of North America, pastors and self-styled prophets often attribute poverty, infertility, addiction, or illness to ancestral sin. This theology of inherited doom merges ancient magical thinking with modern guilt psychology: individuals internalize collective suffering as metaphysical inheritance.[11]

The appeal is obvious. The doctrine absolves people from direct responsibility for their predicament ("It's my family's curse") while preserving moral order by framing suffering as punishment. Yet philosophically it is untenable and ethically catastrophic.

---

11. Asongu, "Prevalence of Superstitious Beliefs."

CHAPTER SIX: REFUTATION OF DESTINY

1. Violation of Realism:

   CSR's first pillar—Metaphysical Realism—requires that claims correspond to observable reality. The generational curse postulate cannot be verified empirically. There is no measurable causal mechanism linking an ancestor's actions to a descendant's misfortune outside biological inheritance or sociocultural conditioning.

2. Collapse of Coherence:

   The doctrine contradicts both empirical genetics and moral logic. Genetics transmits traits, not guilt. Ethics presupposes personal responsibility, not hereditary condemnation. A God who punishes grandchildren for the sins of grandparents would contradict the moral coherence of justice itself (Ezekiel 18:20).

3. Failure of Falsifiability:

   The generational curse is non-falsifiable. Any counter-example can be reinterpreted—prosperity becomes a temporary respite before the curse "returns." As Popper warned,[12] such theories immunize themselves against refutation and thus cease to be rational knowledge.

4. Erosion of Integrity:

   The doctrine breeds exploitation. Religious entrepreneurs monetize deliverance rituals, turning metaphysical despair into financial profit. By preying on fear, they violate the ethical commitment to truth and the protection of the vulnerable.

From the standpoint of CSR, the generational curse is an epistemic crime—a public assertion of unwarranted testimony designed to control others. Its persistence reflects a deeper moral deficit: the replacement of truth-seeking with psychological manipulation.

---

12. Popper, *Logic of Scientific Discovery*.

PART TWO: REFUTATION

6.4.3 Fatalism, Trauma, and the Need for Control

Psychologically, fatalism thrives where trauma and powerlessness coincide. Individuals who have endured chronic oppression—whether under slavery, colonialism, systemic racism, or domestic abuse—often adopt fatalistic beliefs as coping strategies. The narrative "God willed it" converts unbearable chaos into meaningful order.[13] This is understandable, even compassionate, but from a philosophical perspective it represents a transitional rather than ultimate solution.

Trauma researchers describe this phenomenon as *survivor adaptation*: the victim internalizes helplessness to maintain coherence. Yet if unchallenged, this adaptation becomes pathology. The survivor who tells herself that abuse was destined may find solace but forfeits agency; she cannot act to prevent recurrence. At the collective level, post-colonial societies that interpret their subjugation as destiny internalize dependency. Development aid becomes a modern form of penance for a "cursed" past rather than a rational project for systemic change.

CSR reframes healing as epistemic restoration. Recovery requires reconnecting belief to evidence—recognizing that while suffering is real, its meaning is not given but constructed. Freedom arises when individuals reinterpret their pain as data, not destiny: evidence for change, not proof of fate.

6.4.4 The Cognitive Economy of Destiny

Fatalism persists because it is cognitively economical. Thinking critically is effortful; believing in destiny is effortless. To attribute success or failure to fate simplifies complexity and preserves ego. Psychologists call this the *just-world hypothesis*: the tendency to believe that people get what they deserve.[14] It reassures observ-

---

13. Frankl, *Man's Search for Meaning*.
14. Lerner, *Belief in a Just World*.

CHAPTER SIX: REFUTATION OF DESTINY

ers that tragedy will not strike them if they behave properly, but it also legitimates injustice by blaming victims for their misfortune ("Their fate must have required it").

In this way, fatalism functions as an *ideology of emotional convenience*. It replaces causal investigation with moral judgment. Rather than studying systemic factors—bad governance, unequal opportunity, structural discrimination—societies label suffering as destiny, thereby protecting existing hierarchies. CSR exposes this mechanism as epistemic laziness masquerading as virtue. The refusal to analyze complexity is not humility; it is a moral failure of curiosity.

6.4.5 The Neuropsychology of Freedom

Neuroscientific research increasingly supports CSR's claim that freedom is an emergent property of complexity rather than an illusion. While deterministic interpretations of brain activity once suggested that decisions are pre-made before conscious awareness,[15] later studies revealed that consciousness can modify, inhibit, or redirect impulses even milliseconds before action.[16] The brain operates probabilistically, integrating sensory data, memory, and goals to generate multiple possible actions. Choice is the selection among these probabilities.

In this model, freedom is not absolute spontaneity but *adaptive flexibility*—the capacity of a system to alter its own responses in light of new information. CSR interprets this as epistemic freedom: the ability of consciousness to test and revise internal hypotheses about the world. Thus, biological evidence now aligns with philosophical realism: the universe provides constraints, but human intelligence transforms constraints into opportunities.

---

15. Libet, "Unconscious Cerebral Initiative."
16. Schurger et al., "Accumulator Model."

PART TWO: REFUTATION

6.4.6 The Communal Dimension of Fatalism

Fatalism is rarely individual. It is a shared cultural narrative that organizes collective identity. Anthropological studies of peasant communities[17] show that fatalistic proverbs—"What will be, will be"—serve as social lubricants, preventing envy and preserving harmony in hierarchies of scarcity. Such proverbs have survival value in oppressive contexts, yet they also prevent political mobilization. When resignation becomes a virtue, resistance becomes sin.

The CSR framework recognizes the social necessity of stability but argues that genuine cohesion must be grounded in truth, not illusion. A community that builds solidarity on shared resignation cannot evolve; it confuses peace with paralysis. The moral task of intellectuals, educators, and faith leaders is therefore to replace fatalistic solidarity with epistemic solidarity: a shared commitment to truth-testing, problem-solving, and accountability.

6.4.7 The Liberation of Faith

Fatalism must be distinguished from authentic faith. The former abolishes freedom; the latter assumes it. Faith, rightly understood, is trust in the meaningfulness of reality, not the fixity of outcomes. The biblical narrative itself refutes fatalism: Abraham argues with God, Moses defies Pharaoh, the prophets rebuke kings. In each case, moral courage presupposes the capacity to alter history. Jesus' own ethical teaching assumes contingency: "According to your faith be it unto you" (Matthew 9:29). The human response matters.

Liberation theology, particularly in its African and Latin American expressions, reclaims this active faith. As Asongu argues,[18] divine providence must never be used to justify oppression or excuse injustice; revelation calls humanity to co-create justice with God. CSR and liberation theology converge in this respect: both

---

17. Scott, *Moral Economy of the Peasant.*
18. Asongu, "New Frontiers."

affirm that truth is participatory. Reality unfolds through action informed by knowledge.

Thus, the proper theological attitude is not resignation but *responsible hope*: the belief that divine order invites human collaboration through reason and love. In this view, the generational curse dissolves; the only inheritance that binds humanity is the moral obligation to pursue truth.

6.4.8 The Counseling Perspective: From Determinism to Empowerment

Counseling psychology offers practical tools for dismantling fatalistic cognition. Cognitive-behavioral therapy (CBT) demonstrates that emotions follow interpretations; by changing one's explanatory style, one changes one's experience of control.[19] The counselor's task is to help clients re-establish causal agency: to replace global, stable, and uncontrollable attributions ("I always fail because I'm cursed") with specific, temporary, and controllable ones ("I failed this time because I didn't prepare adequately, but I can change that").

Within the CSR framework, counseling becomes a microcosm of epistemic sovereignty. The therapist guides the client through the *Synthetic Loop*: gathering experiential data, testing beliefs against evidence, integrating coherence with personal values, and generating new, falsifiable behavioral hypotheses. The result is liberation—not metaphysical, but psychological and epistemic.

At the social level, educational systems must play the same role. Schools and universities should function as civic counseling spaces where nations collectively re-author their self-narratives. The pedagogy of freedom replaces the pedagogy of fate.

---

19. Beck, *Cognitive Behavior Therapy*.

PART TWO: REFUTATION

6.4.9 The Global Variants of Fatalism

Fatalism's pervasiveness demonstrates its adaptive flexibility. In South Asia, it manifests as karmic resignation; in East Asia, as Confucian acceptance of hierarchical order; in the West, as techno-determinism ("the algorithm made the decision"); and in parts of Africa, as spiritual determinism and ancestral curses. CSR exposes all these as structurally identical: each denies conditional causation and replaces inquiry with submission.

Modern capitalism, too, harbors a secular fatalism. Market fundamentalists speak of "the invisible hand" as if it were an infallible deity. Economic crises are treated as acts of fate rather than failures of policy. Even within scientific discourse, genetic essentialism and AI determinism portray human beings as biochemical or algorithmic puppets.[20] The moral consequence is uniform: reduced responsibility, diminished empathy, and political stagnation.

CSR's antidote is universal: re-establish the link between cause, choice, and consequence. The recognition that "the system can change because its conditions can change" is the intellectual foundation of all progress—from personal therapy to planetary ethics.

6.4.10 Summary: Fatalism as an Epistemic Addiction

In sum, fatalism operates like an addiction. It provides immediate relief from uncertainty but long-term degradation of agency. It is emotionally soothing, socially convenient, and intellectually catastrophic. Under CSR's analysis, fatalism is the archetype of unwarranted belief: a system that cannot be tested, cannot be corrected, and therefore cannot evolve.

The cure lies not in new metaphysics but in renewed courage—the willingness to confront contingency without consolation, to build

---

20. O'Neil, *Weapons of Math Destruction*.

meaning through knowledge rather than myth. Only then can humanity rediscover what destiny truly means: not a script written for us, but a story we write through understanding.

6.5 EPISTEMIC SOVEREIGNTY AND THE ETHICS OF FREEDOM

6.5.1 The Recovery of Epistemic Sovereignty

The final task in refuting destiny is not merely intellectual—it is civilizational. To defeat fatalism, humanity must reclaim epistemic sovereignty, the right and responsibility to generate, test, and act upon warranted knowledge. Epistemic sovereignty is the moral foundation of all other forms of sovereignty. Political independence without epistemic freedom is illusion; technological advancement without epistemic integrity is peril.

In earlier chapters, Critical Synthetic Realism (CSR) was developed as a theory of truth; here, it becomes a theory of liberation. Freedom begins not in revolution but in recognition: the recognition that knowledge is conditional, corrigible, and participatory. This recognition re-opens the closed world of fatalism. It replaces prophecy with probability, decree with discovery, superstition with verification.

To reclaim epistemic sovereignty is to rebuild the Synthetic Loop as a civic institution. Reason must again generate hypotheses; Experience must test them; Coherence must integrate them; and Testimony must report them honestly. These four processes—once internalized by a society—constitute the very infrastructure of freedom. They transform passive believers into active investigators, transforming the idea of destiny into the practice of agency.

PART TWO: REFUTATION

6.5.2 The Ethics of Freedom: Choice as Moral Obligation

Freedom is not simply the ability to choose; it is the obligation to choose responsibly in light of truth. CSR defines this as the Integrity Rule—the moral law that every claim and action must correspond to reality. In this sense, freedom and truth are inseparable: a society that abandons truth inevitably sacrifices liberty, because decisions made on false premises enslave their makers to illusion.

Fatalism violates this moral law by disguising avoidance as acceptance. It allows individuals and communities to evade accountability by invoking metaphysical inevitability. "It was destined" becomes the moral anesthetic for injustice. CSR counters that genuine humility lies not in surrender but in accuracy—acknowledging what is and what can be changed. The ethical essence of agency is this acknowledgment: the courage to see reality as conditional, not cursed.

In practical terms, the Ethics of Freedom require:

1. Truthful Speech: Language must correspond to facts. Public discourse should reward accuracy, not charisma.
2. Evidence-Based Decision-Making: Policy and belief must submit to empirical verification.
3. Transparent Testimony: Authority must justify itself through warranted expertise, not sacred status.
4. Moral Accountability: Individuals and institutions must accept causal responsibility for preventable harm.

Freedom without these norms degenerates into chaos; truth without them calcifies into dogma. Their synthesis—freedom grounded in truth—is the ethical horizon of CSR.

CHAPTER SIX: REFUTATION OF DESTINY

6.5.3 Freedom and Contingency: The New Metaphysics of Hope

A recurring question for theologians and scientists alike is whether freedom requires the universe to be indeterminate. CSR answers more precisely: freedom requires that the universe be *conditionally* *open*—lawful yet contingent. Causality provides structure; contingency provides possibility. Hope lives in the intersection.

Fatalism, in all its guises, seeks escape from contingency. It yearns for certainty, even if that certainty costs meaning. Yet the grandeur of existence lies in its unpredictability. The universe is not a closed equation but a living system of probabilities, constantly rewritten by feedback. To live truthfully is to live experimentally—to accept that we cannot know all outcomes but can improve the conditions that generate them.

This epistemic humility is the highest form of faith. It is not the belief that everything happens for a reason, but that everything happens according to reasons we may yet discover. Such faith transforms destiny from decree into dialogue. The human task is not submission but participation.

6.5.4 Education as the Architecture of Agency

The institutional site of epistemic sovereignty is education. Fatalism thrives where education is authoritarian—when teachers demand recitation rather than reasoning, obedience rather than observation. CSR proposes a new pedagogical model: education as epistemic emancipation.

1. Curriculum Reform: Every subject must be taught as a method of inquiry, not a collection of facts. Students should learn how knowledge is produced, tested, and corrected.

PART TWO: REFUTATION

2. Dialogical Classrooms: The Socratic method must replace the catechism. The teacher becomes a facilitator of the Synthetic Loop, not its terminus.

3. Interdisciplinary Thinking: Realism, Coherence, Experience, and Testimony intersect across domains—science, art, theology, and ethics. Education should reflect that unity.

4. Moral Formation: Students must be taught that truth-telling is not merely academic honesty but civic duty. The courage to correct error is the first act of citizenship.

Education, in this vision, becomes the opposite of indoctrination. It is the systematic training of the mind to resist unwarranted claims, whether they come from prophets, politicians, or algorithms. It transforms the passive consumer of culture into the active constructor of reality.

6.5.5 Faith and Freedom Reconciled

Fatalism has often masqueraded as faith. The two must now be disentangled and reconciled. Faith, in its noblest sense, is trust in the intelligibility and goodness of reality—a confidence that truth is worth seeking and that the universe rewards sincerity. Fatalism, by contrast, is despair disguised as devotion. It denies the very principle of co-creation that makes faith meaningful.

CSR enables this reconciliation by restoring epistemic dignity to belief. A believer can affirm divine providence without surrendering human responsibility, for providence operates through secondary causes—human intelligence, compassion, and creativity. The theologian Jürgen Moltmann called this the "theology of hope": faith not in fixed outcomes, but in the divine invitation to participate in redemption.[21]

Thus, under CSR, reason and revelation are not enemies. Reason is revelation's instrument; revelation is reason's horizon. The

---

21. Moltmann, *Theology of Hope*.

CHAPTER SIX: REFUTATION OF DESTINY

miracle is not that destiny rules the world, but that knowledge can change it.

6.5.6 Governance and the Integrity Rule

The Ethics of Freedom must be institutionalized. Governments are the moral laboratories of a civilization's epistemic values. A state that tolerates lies in its public records or propaganda in its media cannot sustain democracy. The Integrity Rule requires that:

- Policy equals hypothesis: Every public project must define measurable objectives and submit to evaluation.
- Transparency equals verification: Data, budgets, and research must be open to public scrutiny.
- Accountability equals realism: Officials must be judged by outcomes that correspond to stated goals.

When these norms are violated, corruption flourishes, and fatalism returns as cynicism: "That's just how things are." Cynicism is modern fatalism—the belief that systems cannot change. CSR refutes this by demonstrating that institutions are human artifacts; what was built by human choice can be rebuilt by human knowledge.

6.5.7 The Global Dimension: Freedom as Shared Epistemology

Fatalism is not confined to any culture or religion. It thrives wherever systems discourage falsification. In authoritarian states, truth becomes decreed; in populist movements, it becomes emotional; in algorithmic societies, it becomes calculated. The antidote must therefore be universal: a global epistemic ethic grounded in CSR.

This ethic affirms that all human beings participate in the same reality and are therefore bound by the same duty to warrant their claims. Cross-cultural dialogue becomes possible only when interlocutors agree that truth exists and can, however tentatively, be approached through shared evidence.

International institutions—scientific, economic, educational—should embed CSR principles: open data, peer review, falsifiability, and the moral separation of truth from utility. When knowledge is governed by propaganda or profit alone, the world re-enters the darkness of myth, whether under the flag of ideology or the logo of a corporation.

Global peace, therefore, requires epistemic peace: a mutual commitment to reason as humanity's common language.

6.5.8 Freedom and the Splendor of Truth

In the final analysis, fatalism is the shadow cast by the fear of truth. To accept the splendor of truth is to accept responsibility for it—to recognize that knowledge binds as well as liberates. CSR restores the ancient insight of the Greek *aletheia* (unconcealment): that truth is not a static object but a light that exposes our ignorance and demands response.

Freedom is not the absence of limits but the mastery of limits through understanding. When we comprehend the causal structure of reality, we expand the range of what is possible. Every scientific discovery, every moral reform, every act of courage is a refutation of destiny.

The universe is not a closed system of necessity; it is an open conversation between law and liberty. Humanity's greatness lies not in submission to fate but in participation in creation. The future is not written—it is written *with* us.

6.5.9 Conclusion: From Destiny to Responsibility

The refutation of destiny is, ultimately, the affirmation of responsibility. The belief in fate—whether cloaked in theology, biology,

CHAPTER SIX: REFUTATION OF DESTINY

or data—renders humanity passive. CSR reveals that the world is structured for cooperation between knowledge and action. Every law of nature is an invitation to mastery; every mystery, a summons to inquiry.

Generational curses, deterministic algorithms, and cosmic decrees all fail the test of warranted knowledge. They explain nothing, correct nothing, and free no one. They are the ghosts of ignorance, haunting the corridors of human fear. The true "curse" of humanity is not ancestral sin but epistemic complacency—the refusal to think critically about the conditions of our existence.

To live under CSR is to live awake: to treat every claim as a hypothesis, every failure as data, every success as a provisional truth. It is to build civilization not on prophecy but on proof, not on destiny but on discovery. The splendor of truth is not its finality but its luminosity—the light it sheds on our freedom to change.

As Amartya Sen reminds us, development is freedom.[22] We might now add: *Freedom is knowledge.* The task before humanity is clear: to convert belief into understanding, resignation into responsibility, and destiny into deliberate action. In this transformation, the fatalist becomes the philosopher, the believer becomes the builder, and the world becomes, once again, open to possibility.

---

22. Sen, *Development as Freedom.*

CHAPTER SEVEN: THE ETHICS OF EFFORT— RECONCILING CONDITIONAL CAUSALITY AND THE EFFICACY OF PRAYER

This chapter employs the philosophical framework of Critical Synthetic Realism (CSR) to examine the epistemic validity and ethical implications of *Prayer as Mechanism*—the claim that petitionary prayer directly and non-conditionally alters material reality. By applying the Axiological Distinction, the study separates the warranted psychological and social benefits of prayer (*Prayer as Therapy*) from its unwarranted causal claims.

The central critique is articulated through the Answered Prayer Dilemma, which demonstrates that any material outcome following prayer is either epistemologically redundant (caused by pre-existing conditional factors) or unwarrantably miraculous (violating the integrity of causal closure).

CHAPTER SEVEN: THE ETHICS OF EFFORT

Building on this, the chapter introduces Providence Without Partiality: The Ethics of Petition in a Conditional World, examining the incoherence of competitive prayer (for wars, elections, sports, and fortune) in a causally closed universe. CSR concludes that prayer's power is moral and psychological, not mechanical. The true devotion lies not in petition, but in participation—transforming faith into effort. The final *Epilogue: Faith, Effort, and the Silence of Heaven* affirms that, though prayer may not alter physical reality, it remains a legitimate cultural and spiritual practice that sustains moral courage and meaning.

7.1 INTRODUCTION: THE PHILOSOPHICAL TENSION BETWEEN AGENCY AND PETITION

The human spirit has always sought dialogue with the transcendent. Prayer—particularly *petitionary prayer*—is among humanity's oldest and most universal acts. It embodies the hope that thought can influence the world beyond the causal reach of the body, that plea can shape providence. Yet, the same act raises profound epistemic and ethical dilemmas.

If the world operates under consistent causal laws, can prayer—an act of internal will—alter those laws? Can the non-conditional affect the conditional? These questions are not merely theological curiosities but philosophical necessities for any worldview that upholds epistemic integrity and human agency.

Critical Synthetic Realism (CSR) provides a lens for evaluating this question. CSR asserts that all warranted knowledge arises from the disciplined interaction of Reason and Experience, tested through the dynamic loop of coherence, correspondence, and falsifiability. It demands that every claim about the world—material, spiritual, or moral—be evaluated through evidence, logical consistency, and reproducibility.

When examined through this lens, prayer's epistemic status divides cleanly:

- As *psychological experience*, prayer is real, powerful, and measurable.
- As *mechanism of external causation*, prayer is unwarranted by the standards of critical realism.

This distinction need not destroy faith; rather, it refines it. Prayer may comfort the heart, but effort transforms the world. Faith without work, as the Epistle of James reminds us, is dead (James 2:26). The purpose of this chapter is to preserve the dignity of faith by aligning it with truth—to reconcile belief with reason, and devotion with responsibility.

7.2 THE FRAMEWORK OF CRITICAL SYNTHETIC REALISM

Critical Synthetic Realism (CSR)—a philosophical system developed to defend objective truth in an age of epistemic relativism—rests on three interdependent pillars:

1. Realism: There exists an objective, mind-independent reality. Truth corresponds to that reality (*adaequatio intellectus et rei*).
2. Synthesis: Knowledge arises through the systematic integration of four justificatory sources—Reason, Experience, Coherence, and Testimony.
3. Criticality: Knowledge remains provisional, open to falsification and revision through the correction of error.

From these principles emerges the Integrity Rule: all public and private actions must be based on warranted knowledge—claims justified by empirical evidence and rational coherence.

CSR therefore recognizes Conditional Causality as the governing law of the material world: for any effect (E), there exists a discoverable and inspectable chain of material conditions ($C_1, C_2, C_3 \ldots$).

Any claim invoking non-conditional or supernatural causes must meet an even higher standard of warrant, which, so far, none has.

When applied to prayer, this framework differentiates between:

- Prayer as Therapy: internally warranted, psychologically and socially beneficial.
- Prayer as Mechanism: externally unwarranted, violating the law of conditional causation.

7.3 PHILOSOPHICAL JUSTIFICATIONS OF PRAYER

Humanity has never ceased to justify prayer. From metaphysical systems to pragmatic ethics, prayer has been defended as rational, natural, or necessary. CSR does not dismiss these justifications but evaluates their epistemic coherence.

7.3.1 The Metaphysical Justification: Prayer as Divine Causation

Classical theology, from Augustine to Aquinas, conceived prayer as *secondary causation*: God ordains certain outcomes to occur *through* human petition. Aquinas held that prayer "changes not the divine will, but disposes man to receive what God has willed."[1]

This position preserves divine immutability but introduces a contradiction: if prayer can alter which potential outcome is realized, then divine foreknowledge is contingent on human speech—a metaphysical absurdity. CSR concludes that divine providence, if it exists, must operate *through* conditional order, not *against* it. Thus, prayer may align the human will with providence but does not alter the structure of reality.

---

1. Thomas Aquinas, *Summa Theologica* (1947).

PART TWO: REFUTATION

7.3.2 The Psychological Justification: Prayer as Self-Transformation

William James described religious experience as an "energetic tonic" that transforms human character and renews the will to act.[2] Prayer, in this sense, functions as a technology of self-regulation—a psychological therapy that produces measurable benefits.[3]

Neuroscientific studies affirm this: contemplative prayer activates brain regions associated with calm and empathy.[4] Within CSR, these effects are Axiological-I (internal value)—real, measurable, and conditional. They arise from the brain's biochemistry, not divine intervention.

7.3.3 The Phenomenological Justification: Prayer as Encounter

Philosophers such as Martin Buber and Gabriel Marcel framed prayer as *dialogue with being itself*—an "I-Thou" encounter that transcends objectification.[5] This view emphasizes relationship over causation. CSR accepts this as an experiential truth, morally enriching but not empirically causal.

7.3.4 The Pragmatic Justification: Prayer as Moral Practice

William James's pragmatism evaluates religion by its "fruits, not its roots." If prayer fosters courage or altruism, it has moral utility.[6] John Dewey reinterpreted prayer as poetic idealism—the verbal

---

2. James, *Varieties of Religious Experience*.
3. Koenig, "Religion, Spirituality, and Health."
4. Newberg and D'Aquili, *Why God Won't Go Away*.
5. Buber, *I and Thou*.
6. James, *Varieties of Religious Experience*.

enactment of moral aspiration.[7] CSR appreciates this as ethical symbolism, but reminds us: utility is not warrant. A comforting belief is not necessarily a true belief.

7.3.5 The Linguistic Justification: Prayer as Expression

Ludwig Wittgenstein treated prayer as a "form of life"—a linguistic practice expressing value rather than asserting fact.[8] When one prays, "Help me, O God," one expresses dependence, not physics. CSR integrates this linguistic insight: prayer's semantic function is expressive, not causal. Its truth lies in meaning, not in mechanism.

7.3.6 CSR's Synthesis: Prayer Transforms the Subject, Not the Structure

CSR synthesizes these traditions in a single maxim:

"Prayer transforms the subject, not the structure of reality."

The act of prayer reorders the mind, regulates emotion, and strengthens ethical will. These are real changes, grounded in neuropsychological causality. But prayer does not rearrange atoms, alter rainfall, or vote in elections. Its power is internal coherence, not external causation.

7.4 THE ANSWERED PRAYER DILEMMA: THE CRISIS OF CAUSALITY

CSR frames the classic problem of divine intervention as the Answered Prayer Dilemma—the epistemological impossibility of distinguishing answered prayer from coincidence.

---

7. Dewey, *Common Faith*.
8. Wittgenstein, *Philosophical Investigations*.

PART TWO: REFUTATION

7.4.1 Scenario A: The Mundane Answer (Epistemic Redundancy)

Most "answered prayers" occur within natural probability ranges: an illness resolves, an exam is passed, or a storm ends. These events already possess sufficient conditional causes. To attribute them to prayer adds no explanatory power and violates *Occam's Razor*.[9] The simplest warranted explanation—conditional causation—remains the most rational.

7.4.2 Scenario B: The Miraculous Answer (Epistemic Unwarrantability)

When prayer appears to produce outcomes that defy known laws, it becomes epistemically unwarrantable. As Hume argued, it is always more probable that testimony errs than that natural law has been violated.[10] CSR concurs: any claim immune to falsification is excluded from warranted knowledge. Miracles may comfort the believer, but they do not constitute knowledge—they remain private conviction, not public truth.

7.5 THE ETHICAL HAZARD OF DISPLACED ACTION

7.5.1 Abdication of Responsibility

CSR defines epistemic responsibility as a moral obligation. When prayer replaces action, the believer surrenders agency. To pray for a sick child but refuse medical treatment is not piety but negligence. To pray for peace while avoiding justice is hypocrisy.

---

9. Russell, *Problems of Philosophy*.
10. Hume, *Enquiry Concerning Human Understanding*.

Nozick notes that genuine ethics demands bearing the weight of consequence.[11] CSR radicalizes this: faith becomes immoral when it replaces effort.

7.5.2 Misallocation of Resources

When societies devote vast resources to ritual prayer but neglect science, education, or governance, they institutionalize epistemic inefficiency. Devereux calls this the "psychopathology of culture": belief systems that reward symbolic action over causal intervention.[12] The moral failure of such societies lies not in their piety but in their epistemic misalignment—investing in metaphysical speculation while neglecting material responsibility.

7.6 WORK AS RATIONAL DEVOTION: THE TRUE ETHICS OF EFFORT

CSR rehabilitates *work*—rational, disciplined engagement with the conditional world—as the highest expression of spiritual integrity.

To work is to cooperate with reality. The scientist, the farmer, the teacher, and the builder all engage in acts of *conditional creation*. They do not wait for manna; they cultivate the field. This is prayer as participation, not petition.

Work embodies faith in a lawful universe. It is an act of worship because it affirms the order and intelligibility of creation. The Latin monastic maxim *ora et labora*—"pray and work"—captures this synthesis.

Thus, to work well is to pray truthfully.

---

11. Nozick, *Philosophical Explanations*.
12. Devereux, *Ethnopsychiatry*.

PART TWO: REFUTATION

7.7 PROVIDENCE WITHOUT PARTIALITY: THE ETHICS OF PETITION IN A CONDITIONAL WORLD

7.7.1 The Epistemic Contradiction

Petitionary prayer collapses into contradiction when two opposing groups seek divine favor for incompatible outcomes. When two armies, teams, or political factions each pray for victory, the causal logic of prayer becomes incoherent. CSR calls this the Conflict of Invocation: either God arbitrarily chooses sides or natural causality decides the outcome.

The second explanation—skill, preparation, probability—remains epistemically sufficient. The first makes God a partisan, undermining divine justice.

7.7.2 The Ethical Absurdity of Divine Favoritism

If divine power determines earthly competitions, then moral coherence dissolves. Why would God grant victory in football or politics while ignoring famine and genocide? Such a theology transforms God into a celestial broker of vanity. CSR rejects this as *anthropomorphic projection*—the projection of tribal psychology onto metaphysics.

7.7.3 The Psychological Reality: Prayer as Performance

Group prayer in competitive contexts functions as *collective psychotechnology*: it bonds communities, reduces anxiety, and sharpens focus. The efficacy is psychological, not supernatural. CSR affirms this internal power but insists that it leaves external causality untouched.

CHAPTER SEVEN: THE ETHICS OF EFFORT

7.7.4 The Theological Reinterpretation: General Providence

The only rational theism compatible with CSR is *general providence*: God sustains the order of causality but does not suspend it arbitrarily. Divine goodness manifests as the reliability of natural law, not its violation.

Thus, prayer's true power is alignment—conforming human intention to cosmic order, not attempting to manipulate it.

7.7.5 CSR's Resolution: Providence Through Participation

CSR resolves the tension: divine providence operates *through* conditional causality. The "miracle" is not that prayer changes events, but that it changes the agent who changes events. Providence is cooperative, not competitive.

In this sense, God's favor lies not on those who pray most, but on those who work most faithfully within truth. The divine will is not an override of causality but its moral completion.

7.8 THE COMPASSION OF REALISM AND THE HUMILITY OF DOUBT

CSR's critique of prayer's external efficacy is not an assault on faith but an act of intellectual compassion. The purpose is to preserve truth from sentimentality, not to rob hope of meaning.

The Answered Prayer Dilemma demonstrates that every claimed miracle is either conditionally explicable or epistemically indeterminate. Yet this realization does not render prayer meaningless—it relocates its meaning. Prayer becomes a dialogue with uncertainty, an act of existential courage in a contingent world.

The wise believer, therefore, prays not for outcomes but for clarity, not for victory but for virtue. As Socrates prayed, "Grant that I may be beautiful within." The mature faith is not childish dependence but disciplined fidelity to reality.

7.9 EPILOGUE: FAITH, EFFORT, AND THE SILENCE OF HEAVEN

The author must end this inquiry as a Christian philosopher—with reverence, honesty, and humility. To question the *mechanism* of prayer is not to reject its *meaning*.

Scripture itself unites faith and action: "Show me your faith without deeds, and I will show you my faith by my deeds" (James 2:18, NIV). The saints have long understood that work is the tangible expression of belief. The Latin wisdom *ora et labora*—to pray is to work—and the moral proverb *cleanliness is next to godliness* both affirm that moral order, discipline, and labor are themselves acts of devotion.

Even so, human experience forces uncomfortable reflections. We have seen worshippers murdered in churches, synagogues, and mosques; children drowned in floods that destroyed temples; faithful congregations obliterated by earthquakes. In these moments, divine protection appears absent. If God intervenes selectively, His criteria are hidden; if He does not, then the moral weight of care falls to us—to prevent, to rebuild, to console.

Perhaps this is not divine neglect but divine delegation. The silence of heaven is not cruelty; it is a summons. It calls us to act.

Thus, this critique does not discourage prayer. It discourages only the illusion that prayer alone suffices. I will continue to pray—for wisdom, for courage, for serenity—but I will not confuse hope with hydraulics. The world changes through hands guided by wisdom, not wishes.

CHAPTER SEVEN: THE ETHICS OF EFFORT

Prayer, in its truest sense, aligns us with the moral order of the universe; it does not exempt us from the labor it requires. The miracle is not that God answers our words, but that He trusts us enough to let *our work* become the answer.

PART THREE: AGENCY—BUILDING THE RATIONAL SOCIETY AND THE GOOD LIFE

CHAPTER EIGHT: POLITICAL PHILOSOPHY—A DEFENSE OF DEMOCRACY

8.1 INTRODUCTION: THE POLITICAL ARCHITECTURE OF WARRANTED TRUTH

All philosophy ultimately faces the question of governance. Having established in previous chapters that the pursuit of truth requires epistemic humility and continuous self-correction, we must now ask: *what political order best sustains the pursuit of warranted truth in the public sphere?*

Critical Synthetic Realism (CSR) teaches that all human knowledge is provisional, conditional, and correctable. The moral duty of the rational agent is to participate actively in this process of correction—by testing, revising, and improving the shared structures of thought that govern collective life. In the political domain, this moral duty translates into the search for a system that institutionalizes *falsifiability*: a government capable of correcting itself without violence, capable of learning from experience, and willing to subordinate ideology to evidence.

This chapter argues that democracy—properly understood and continually reformed—is not merely a preference for equality or freedom; it is the epistemic embodiment of the Synthetic Loop. Democracy is reason made social: it operationalizes the scientific virtues of testing, refutation, and correction within the moral framework of civic life.

We shall examine the social contract tradition that gave birth to modern democracy, critique the epistemic weaknesses of existing democratic systems (especially the United States), and propose the contours of a new democratic ideal—the Epistemic Republic—which fully aligns with the principles of CSR.

8.2 DEMOCRACY AS INSTITUTIONALIZED FALSIFIABILITY

At the heart of democracy lies an elegant epistemological insight: all power must be subject to falsification. Political authority, like any scientific theory, is a hypothesis about what works best in the conditional world. If its predictions fail—if its policies produce suffering or stagnation—it must be revised or replaced.

In a rational polity, laws and policies function as hypotheses. Elections, accountability mechanisms, and public discourse form the *experiment*. Citizens are not merely voters; they are the data points of collective experience, the living instruments of empirical feedback.

8.2.1 The Political Synthetic Loop

The political Synthetic Loop mirrors CSR's structure:

1. Hypothesis (Reason): Policymakers propose actions based on theory or ideology.
2. Experiment (Experience): The policies are implemented, producing measurable social and economic outcomes.
3. Testing (Criticality): Citizens, institutions, and media evaluate whether the outcomes correspond to the promises.

4. Correction (Falsification): Through elections, judicial review, or civil protest, failed hypotheses are rejected and replaced.

A democratic society thus institutionalizes the permanent *right to be wrong*—and the higher responsibility to correct one's errors. Its genius is not perfection, but adaptability.

8.2.2 Democracy as a Self-Correction Engine

Karl Popper argued that democracy's value lies less in selecting perfect rulers than in *removing bad ones without bloodshed*.[1] In epistemic terms, democracy minimizes the duration and intensity of collective error. Totalitarian regimes can sustain falsehoods for generations; democracy, through regular elections and a free press, subjects every governing claim to the experiment of experience.

From a CSR standpoint, democracy is the only known system that aligns the structure of governance with the structure of truth. Every four or five years, the polity performs a collective act of falsification, testing whether power still corresponds to reality.

8.3 THE SOCIAL CONTRACT AND THE EPISTEMIC COVENANT

The philosophical foundation of democracy rests upon the social contract: the voluntary association of rational beings under rules that secure peace and mutual benefit. Yet CSR reveals that traditional contract theory must be re-interpreted as an *epistemic covenant*: a collective agreement not only to coexist, but to seek truth together.

---

1. Popper, *Conjectures and Refutations*.

PART THREE: AGENCY

8.3.1 Hobbes, Locke, and Rousseau Revisited

- Hobbes envisioned the contract as an escape from chaos. In *Leviathan*, citizens surrender their judgment to an absolute sovereign in exchange for security. But this arrangement abolishes the Synthetic Loop: once truth is decreed, it can no longer be tested. Hobbes's state is a static monolith—a structure of obedience, not inquiry.
- Locke replaced fear with *reason*. In *Two Treatises of Government* (1689), the people retain natural rights and authorize government as their rational instrument. Locke's system anticipates CSR by asserting that legitimate authority arises from evidence-based consent.
- Rousseau, in *The Social Contract* (1762), sought moral unity in the "general will."[2] Yet the general will risks becoming a metaphysical absolute—immune to correction once declared. CSR therefore modifies Rousseau's vision by grounding collective will in falsifiability: the will of the people must be continuously tested against experience.

8.3.2 The Veil of Error: A New Construct

John Rawls proposed the *veil of ignorance* to ensure fairness in designing society.[3] CSR introduces a complementary idea: the *veil of error*. Because human cognition is fallible, all governance must assume that its own beliefs are incomplete or mistaken. The veil of error mandates epistemic humility as a constitutional principle. It converts uncertainty from a weakness into a safeguard: laws must be written to allow their own revision.

This leads to an upgraded form of the social contract: the Epistemic Covenant—a collective promise that no claim, institution,

---

2. Rousseau, *Contrat social*.
3. Rawls, *Theory of Justice*.

or leader is beyond scrutiny; that every authority remains accountable to the empirical reality of the people's lived experience.

8.4 DOCTRINES OF DEMOCRACY: COMPETING MODELS AND THEIR LIMITS

To strengthen democracy, we must examine rival systems and doctrines through the CSR lens, measuring how well each sustains the Synthetic Loop.

8.4.1 Utilitarianism and the Tyranny of Numbers

Utilitarianism reduces politics to the maximization of aggregate happiness.[4] While pragmatic, it often collapses the Integrity Rule: truth becomes secondary to perceived utility. A democracy guided solely by utility risks justifying injustice if it pleases the majority. CSR insists that *truth precedes utility*: policy must first correspond to reality, then serve the good.

8.4.2 Marxism and the Problem of Historical Certitude

Marxism's moral critique of exploitation is valid, but its epistemic flaw lies in its deterministic certainty—the belief that history unfolds through inevitable material laws. When Marxist states seized power, they claimed final truth about social dynamics, abolishing falsifiability. In CSR terms, this was an epistemic heresy: the theory became unfalsifiable dogma, transforming reason into ideology.

---

4. Bentham, *Principles of Morals and Legislation.*

PART THREE: AGENCY

8.4.3 Libertarianism and the Myth of Perfect Autonomy

Libertarianism errs in the opposite direction. By privatizing truth—treating each individual's perception as sovereign—it dissolves the coherence necessary for collective inquiry. The absence of shared verification mechanisms leaves the public sphere vulnerable to disinformation and plutocratic control.

8.4.4 Feminist and Communitarian Correctives

Feminist epistemology[5] and communitarian thought[6] provide necessary correctives. They remind us that knowledge is situated and that empathy—attention to marginalized experience—is itself an epistemic virtue. CSR integrates this insight by defining Distributed Epistemic Sensitivity: the principle that every group must have the means to contribute data and critique to the social experiment. Inclusion is not charity; it is accuracy.

8.5 DIAGNOSING THE AMERICAN EXPERIMENT

The United States remains the world's most influential democracy, yet it exhibits structural flaws that now threaten its epistemic integrity. Each deviation from the CSR model diminishes its capacity for warranted self-correction.

8.5.1 The Senate: Arithmetic Injustice

The U.S. Senate grants two votes to each state regardless of population. Wyoming's 600,000 citizens wield the same legislative power as California's 39 million—a violation of proportional Coherence. The result is *epistemic distortion*: national policies

---

5. Harding, *Whose Science?*
6. Etzioni, *Spirit of Community.*

emerge not from aggregate reality but from a statistical mirage. In CSR terms, this is a systemic falsification error—the data sample of democracy is biased at its core.

8.5.2 The Electoral College and the Mirage of Majority

The Electoral College similarly converts minority preferences into decisive power. In 2000 and 2016, presidents assumed office despite losing the popular vote. Such outcomes undermine Realism: they create a formal truth (legal victory) that contradicts empirical reality (majority choice). CSR demands reform—either proportional allocation or abolition—to restore correspondence between claim and fact.

8.5.3 The Presidency: Reverence Without Accountability

No American president has ever been imprisoned after leaving office, not because all were virtuous, but because cultural reverence shields them. This reverence violates the Integrity Rule. In contrast, France and South Korea routinely prosecute former presidents, demonstrating a higher tolerance for falsification. The CSR reform would equalize the presidency before the law, affirming that power earns reverence only through performance, not office.

8.5.4 Representation Without Representation

The slogan "Taxation without representation" still applies to Washington, D.C., Puerto Rico, Guam, and other territories whose citizens serve, pay, and die for the republic without full legislative voice. This epistemic exclusion contradicts the very experiment of democracy. CSR therefore argues for statehood or proportional representation for all U.S. territories—truth and justice demand inclusion in the dataset of governance.

PART THREE: AGENCY

8.5.5 Money, Media, and the Collapse of Testimony

Corporate money distorts political testimony. When lobbyists and donors outweigh citizens, the evidence considered by government ceases to correspond to public reality. Similarly, polarized media ecosystems create "epistemic silos," breaking national Coherence. CSR demands transparency in campaign finance and algorithmic accountability in media dissemination to restore factual unity.

8.5.6 Lifetime Tenure and Judicial Rigidity

The U.S. Supreme Court's lifetime appointments risk epistemic ossification. The justices' decisions, often shaped by decades-old ideologies, may remain immune to new evidence. CSR recommends renewable terms with mandatory review mechanisms—a judicial falsifiability clause—to ensure the Court evolves with empirical and moral progress.

8.6 SEPARATION OF CHURCH AND STATE: THE EPISTEMIC BOUNDARY

Democracy must operate within the conditional realm of warranted truth. Religion belongs to the transcendent realm of faith—valuable for meaning, but unwarrantable as policy. The American Founders intuited this principle in the First Amendment, but its epistemic rationale was never fully articulated. CSR provides that rationale.

Faith, by its nature, is non-falsifiable. To legislate it is to violate the Synthetic Loop. When religion dictates policy—whether on science education, reproductive rights, or minority inclusion—the state replaces conditional causality with metaphysical decree. *Engel v. Vitale* (1962) and *Lemon v. Kurtzman* (1971) recognized this: government may neither establish religion nor inhibit its private practice.

CHAPTER EIGHT: POLITICAL PHILOSOPHY

CSR reframes this as the Principle of Epistemic Separation: public law must remain confined to propositions that can be empirically or logically warranted. Faith may inspire individual virtue, but it cannot function as public evidence. This protects both religion (from politicization) and science (from sanctification), maintaining the integrity of both domains.

8.7 THE EPISTEMIC REPUBLIC: DEMOCRACY FOR THE AGE OF COMPLEXITY

If democracy is the political form of the Synthetic Loop, then the modern world—dominated by AI, data, and global interdependence—demands an evolved version: the Epistemic Republic.

8.7.1 The Four Pillars of the Epistemic Republic

1. Truth Infrastructure: Establish public institutions tasked with verifying claims—*Public Falsifiability Offices* and *Integrity Auditors* that test government reports, media narratives, and policy outcomes against empirical data.

2. Transparency Mandate: Require that all significant political, financial, and algorithmic processes be inspectable, reproducible, and open to public review.

3. Participatory Knowledge Systems: Implement citizen-science models, deliberative forums, and participatory budgeting to integrate collective experience into decision-making.

4. Integrity Index: Develop measurable indicators of epistemic health—truthfulness of officials, transparency of institutions, resistance to misinformation.

8.7.2 Digital Democracy and Algorithmic Accountability

Algorithms now mediate discourse. To preserve the Synthetic Loop, citizens must know how digital systems shape perception. CSR calls for *Algorithmic Falsifiability*: mandatory disclosure of data sources, weighting criteria, and correction mechanisms. Platforms should be treated as epistemic utilities, obligated to maintain coherence between representation and reality.

8.8 THE GLOBAL DIMENSION: PLANETARY DEMOCRACY

Modern challenges—climate change, pandemics, AI governance—transcend borders. The CSR view recognizes that truth itself is global: atmospheric chemistry and viral transmission obey no national boundaries. The next stage of political evolution must therefore be a Planetary Social Contract, grounded in shared epistemic standards rather than cultural supremacy.

International institutions like the United Nations must evolve from arenas of rhetoric to laboratories of falsifiable policy—testing solutions, publishing results, and revising strategies collectively. The *Epistemic Republic* is scalable: what works for the polis must eventually work for the planet.

8.9 THE ETHICAL FOUNDATION: TRUTH, RESPONSIBILITY, AND FREEDOM

Democracy is not only a political arrangement; it is a moral discipline. It demands citizens who are willing to question their own convictions and leaders who understand that doubt is not weakness but virtue. CSR defines freedom as *the capacity to act upon warranted truth*. A democracy that values emotion over evidence

CHAPTER EIGHT: POLITICAL PHILOSOPHY

or loyalty over logic degenerates into populist mysticism—a regression to collective superstition.

The ethical citizen of the Epistemic Republic must therefore embody three virtues:

1. Intellectual Honesty—refusing to affirm what one knows is unwarranted;
2. Civic Courage—speaking truth to power despite personal cost;
3. Epistemic Humility—recognizing that all human truth is conditional and corrigible.

8.10 TOWARD THE PERFECTIBLE DEMOCRACY: THE BEST THEORY SO FAR

The best theory of democracy in the CSR framework integrates the strengths of the social contract, deliberative democracy, and scientific method into one system of continuous improvement. Its guiding axiom is simple:

No authority is final, and no error is permanent, so long as truth remains public.

The perfectible democracy thus exhibits six essential characteristics:

1. Universal Inclusion—every affected person has epistemic standing;
2. Evidence-Based Policy—decisions require public warrant;
3. Periodic Falsification—regular elections and independent audits;
4. Transparent Algorithms—clarity on digital mediation of truth;
5. Institutional Accountability—all offices subject to empirical review;

6. Global Responsibility—recognition of planetary interdependence.

This model fulfills the Enlightenment promise without the arrogance of infallibility. It treats democracy not as an achievement but as a living method—humanity's collective experiment in truth.

8.11 CONCLUSION: LIBERAL DEMOCRACY AS REASON MADE SOCIAL

The defense of democracy is, in the end, the defense of human reason against despair, ideology, and dogma. A just government is not one that claims to be right, but one that builds mechanisms to discover when it is wrong.

Liberal democracy, when continuously reformed through the lens of CSR, represents the highest form of collective rationality yet achieved. It is the political translation of the scientific spirit—the willingness to test, to fail, and to begin again. Its task is unfinished because the human quest for truth is unfinished.

The promise of democracy is not perfection but correction. It is the only system honest enough to live within the limits of our knowledge, compassionate enough to share power among equals, and courageous enough to confront error without fear. It is, in the fullest sense, *Reason Made Social*.

***

INTERLUDE: THE EPISTEMIC REPUBLIC MANIFESTO

A Reflection on Truth, Freedom, and the Good Life

> "*The freedom to err is the condition of all progress.*"
> — Karl Popper, *The Open Society and Its Enemies* (1945)

CHAPTER EIGHT: POLITICAL PHILOSOPHY

The political is never merely procedural; it is moral. The defense of democracy is not only the defense of votes and laws, but the defense of the human soul's right to seek truth without fear. The *Epistemic Republic* envisioned in the preceding chapter is not a bureaucratic contrivance but a moral covenant—an agreement that the state shall serve truth, and that truth shall, in turn, preserve human dignity.

A democracy worthy of its name is not a marketplace of whims; it is an architecture of inquiry. Its laws are hypotheses, its elections experiments, and its institutions instruments for the continuous refinement of collective knowledge. When it succeeds, it transforms citizens into co-investigators in the great project of human flourishing.

Yet democracy's deepest purpose is not governance—it is growth. It educates the species in humility, teaching that truth is larger than ideology and that no authority, however eloquent, is infallible. The *Epistemic Republic* is thus not the end of politics but its purification: a system designed not to secure victory, but to sustain honesty.

In this light, three moral foundations sustain the link between epistemic order and the good life:

1. Truth as Shared Integrity

   Truth is not possession but covenant. It binds us to the real and to each other, requiring that we speak of the world as it is, not as we wish it to be. To honor truth together is to honor the dignity of reason in all persons. Where lies multiply, freedom dies, for one cannot choose rightly in the dark.

2. Freedom as the Condition of Correction

   Freedom is not chaos but the air in which learning breathes. The free person, like the honest scientist, must live in perpetual readiness to revise. To be free is to risk being wrong;

to remain free is to admit it. In every open debate and lawful protest, the republic rehearses its moral courage.

3. Justice as Epistemic Fairness

Justice is not only the fair distribution of goods but the fair distribution of truth's instruments—education, information, and participation. A society that withholds knowledge commits epistemic violence; it robs citizens not only of power but of reality itself. The first duty of justice, therefore, is to make the truth accessible.

When these principles converge, politics transcends administration and becomes a discipline of virtue. The state that institutionalizes truth, freedom, and justice becomes a living school of moral formation. Its citizens do not merely obey laws; they cultivate wisdom. Its leaders do not command; they learn. Its disagreements are not wars but experiments.

Thus, the true purpose of democracy is not victory but verification—not the rule of numbers but the rule of warranted reason. The just society is one in which knowledge and conscience grow together, where the intellect is not divorced from compassion, and the will to know is married to the will to do good.

The next chapter turns inward—from the external architecture of the rational state to the internal architecture of the ethical soul. If the *Epistemic Republic* represents reason made social, then ethics represents reason made tender. To live well, like to govern well, is to test one's own desires against reality, to refine impulse into virtue, and to transform understanding into love.

For in the end, truth and goodness are not two quests but one: the outer justice of the state and the inner harmony of the soul reflect the same eternal light—the *splendor of truth.*

CHAPTER NINE: THE ARCHITECTURE OF FLOURISHING—FAIRNESS, LOVE, AND THE ETHICS OF THE GOOD SOCIETY

9.1 INTRODUCTION—THE TELEOLOGY OF WARRANTED ACTION

Every philosophy that begins with knowledge must end with ethics. The pursuit of truth, while often treated as an intellectual exercise, is ultimately a moral discipline: a lifelong practice of aligning belief, action, and reality. As the framework of *Critical Synthetic Realism* (CSR) has shown throughout this work, human progress depends upon the Synthetic Loop—the continuous testing and correction of hypotheses through the interplay of *Reason* and *Experience*.[1]

Yet the final purpose of that loop is not accuracy alone but moral coherence. A mind that seeks truth must also seek goodness, for error harms both knowledge and life. In this closing constructive chapter, we therefore ask: *What does a life aligned with reality*

---

1. Popper, *Logic of Scientific Discovery*; Dewey, *Quest for Certainty*.

look like? And more broadly, what political and social order best supports such alignment?

The answer, developed here, is that the Good Life—what Aristotle called *Eudaimonia*[2]—is achieved when individuals and societies live according to the same epistemic virtues that produce warranted knowledge: humility, fairness, compassion, and corrective reason. Flourishing is not a gift but a continuous ethical achievement, and the Good Society is the collective architecture that sustains it.

9.2 EUDAIMONIA—THE HARMONY OF TRUTH, FREEDOM, AND VIRTUE

Aristotle defined *Eudaimonia* as rational activity in accordance with virtue. CSR updates this classical insight: flourishing is the dynamic harmony of *truth* (Realism), *freedom* (Agency), and *virtue* (Epistemic Responsibility).

1. Truth (Realism). The flourishing agent recognizes conditional causality: that every effect requires verifiable causes. Ignorance or superstition are thus ethical failures, because they misalign the self with reality.[3]
2. Freedom (Agency). True freedom is the capacity to generate warranted hypotheses and act upon them. It is both epistemic—the right to know—and political—the right to act.[4]
3. Virtue (Epistemic Responsibility). Virtue lies in submitting one's beliefs to the test of experience, revising them when they fail. This humility before truth is the moral essence of rational life.[5]

When these three converge, life becomes a continuous project of warranted correction. Success brings joy; failure brings data.

2. Aristotle, *Nicomachean Ethics*.
3. Kant, *Critique of Pure Reason*.
4. Sen, *Development as Freedom*.
5. Popper, *Logic of Scientific Discovery*.

CHAPTER NINE: THE ARCHITECTURE OF FLOURISHING

Eudaimonia thus differs from pleasure (*Hedonia*): it is not a state but a process, the serenity that arises from disciplined alignment with reality.

9.3 REDEFINING FAIRNESS—FROM EQUALITY TO EQUITY

9.3.1 Equality and Its Limits

Modern discourse often confuses equality with fairness. Equality gives everyone the same share; fairness demands that outcomes correspond to warranted effort and genuine need.[6] Because individuals begin from unequal conditions—of birth, education, health—identical treatment perpetuates inherited advantage. CSR therefore grounds justice in equity, not sameness. Equity is conditional fairness: adjusting inputs so that every person can participate in the Synthetic Loop of progress.

9.3.2 Equity as Conditional Fairness

A fair society must dismantle epistemic barriers—poverty, ignorance, censorship—that prevent citizens from engaging reality directly. This requires systemic access to information, education, and healthcare.[7] Such access is not charity but the epistemic infrastructure of freedom.

In CSR terms, fairness means:

- Accessible Inputs → Universal education and transparent institutions;
- Warranted Effort → Citizens succeed or fail by the coherence of their action with reality, not by inherited privilege;

---

6. Rawls, *Theory of Justice.*
7. Nussbaum, *Upheavals of Thought.*

- Accountable Outcomes → Policies are judged by empirical results, not rhetoric.

Equity equalizes *conditions* for inquiry, enabling citizens to test their own hypotheses of life. Only then does merit become meaningful.

9.4 SUSTAINABILITY AND INTERGENERATIONAL JUSTICE

9.4.1 Conditional Causality Across Time

Ethics extended through time becomes sustainability. If conditional causality means today's actions shape tomorrow's outcomes, then justice across generations demands stewardship.[8] Exploiting finite ecosystems for short-term gain violates the Integrity Rule—it asserts unwarranted claims about endless growth. Ecological collapse, therefore, is not simply economic failure but epistemic arrogance: denial of natural law.

9.4.2 Regenerative Design—Beyond Maintenance

Where sustainability aims to *sustain*, regenerative design seeks to *restore*. It builds systems—agriculture, architecture, commerce—that enrich rather than exhaust their environments.[9] A regenerative society mirrors the Synthetic Loop: it observes degradation (data), tests corrective innovations, and scales those that work.

Intergenerational fairness thus requires three principles:

1. Transparent Accounting of ecological costs;
2. Restorative Technology that rebuilds natural capital;
3. Education that cultivates ecological literacy as moral literacy.

---

8. Sachs, *Age of Sustainable Development*.
9. Fullerton, *Regenerative Capitalism*.

CHAPTER NINE: THE ARCHITECTURE OF FLOURISHING

To consume without regeneration is to steal from the unborn; to restore is to practice truth over time.

9.5 LOVE AND COMPASSION—THE RATIONAL HEART OF ETHICS

9.5.1 Love as Epistemic Acceptance

Love, properly understood, is reason's gentlest expression—the recognition of shared provisionality. Each person is an unfinished experiment. To love is to accept another's conditional nature and defend their agency to learn, err, and grow.[10] Warranted love refuses to idealize; it aligns compassion with truth.

9.5.2 Warranted Grace

Compassion without justice is indulgence; justice without compassion is cruelty. Warranted Grace unites them. Because all knowledge is provisional, humane systems must permit correction rather than impose final condemnation.[11] Rehabilitation replaces vengeance; education replaces exclusion; mercy becomes the policy of realism.

A society that practices warranted grace refuses to waste human potential. It recognizes that error is inevitable but that ignorance is curable through truth and kindness.

9.6 HAPPINESS—THE SPLENDOR OF ALIGNMENT WITH REALITY

Happiness in CSR is *epistemic peace*: the joy of coherence between belief and world. Anxiety arises from cognitive dissonance—the

---

10. Nussbaum, *Upheavals of Thought*.
11. Arendy, *Human Condition*.

gap between unwarranted hope and empirical fact.[12] The warranted mind minimizes this gap. It fears only self-deception. Failures become feedback; success, temporary harmony.

This condition, akin to Aristotle's *energeia*, is the emotion of truth. It is not the pleasure of having but the satisfaction of *becoming*—the continual renewal of coherence. When knowledge triumphs over illusion, the individual experiences the Splendor of Truth: serenity as the natural light of understanding.

9.7 THE ETHICS OF THE GOOD SOCIETY

Flourishing individuals require flourishing structures. CSR extends moral realism into political design: fairness, kindness, and sustainability must be embedded institutionally.

9.7.1 Epistemic Equity and Universal Education

Education is the social mechanism of warranted knowledge. Following Dewey,[13] a democratic society must treat every school as a laboratory of inquiry. Curricula should teach method over dogma—how to test, not what to believe. The epistemically literate citizen can detect propaganda, challenge corruption, and innovate responsibly. Universal access to such education equalizes the starting line of the Synthetic Loop.

9.7.2 Global Cooperation and Technological Ethics

In a world of AI and algorithmic governance, truth now circulates through machines.[14] CSR demands transparency and human oversight: algorithms must be falsifiable, explainable, and aligned with

---

12. Festinger, *Theory of Cognitive Dissonance*.
13. Dewey, *Democracy and Education*.
14. Bender et al., "Dangers of Stochastic Parrots."

human well-being.[15] Global cooperation on digital ethics becomes the new frontier of justice, ensuring that knowledge remains a public good, not a private weapon.

9.7.3 Integrating Kindness—Beyond Legalism

Law constrains wrongdoing; kindness restores meaning. The Good Society institutionalizes *warranted grace*: welfare systems that buffer failure without eroding responsibility, restorative justice that corrects rather than condemns,[16] and healthcare that treats mental as well as physical suffering. Community becomes the collective epistemic buffer, enabling citizens to re-enter the loop of growth.

9.7.4 Sustainability and Regenerative Civic Design

Urban planning must embody regenerative ethics. Singapore's adaptive greenery, Copenhagen's cycling infrastructure, and Curitiba's integrated transport systems illustrate how cities can learn from feedback—policy as hypothesis, environment as data.[17] Such design transforms sustainability from slogan to structure.

7.5 Synthesis—Principles of the Good Society

Principle	Core Concept	Social Manifestation
Fairness	Conditional Causality	Justice, Accountability, Equalized Opportunity
Kindness/Love	Compassionate Correction	Rehabilitation, Welfare, Warranted Grace
Sustainability	Intergenerational Fairness	Regenerative Design, Environmental Stewardship

15. O'Neil, *Weapons of Math Destruction*.
16. Braithwaite, *Crime, Shame and Reintegration*.
17. Sachs, *Age of Sustainable Development*.

PART THREE: AGENCY

The Good Society is a living hypothesis—constantly tested and refined. Its highest law is the Integrity Rule: that all claims, from budget to belief, must correspond with reality.

9.8 APPLIED ETHICS—JUSTICE AND REGENERATION

9.8.1 Warranted Justice

Punishment detached from correction is epistemically irrational. Comparative studies show that restorative systems—such as Norway's rehabilitation-based model—achieve lower recidivism than purely punitive regimes.[18] Justice aligned with CSR seeks reintegration, not revenge. Each sentence is a social experiment: does it restore agency, deter harm, and sustain fairness? Data, not anger, must decide.

9.8.2 The Regenerative City

Cities concentrate both human creativity and ecological strain. A regenerative city treats its infrastructure as a circulatory system of truth and care.[19] Policies are falsifiable; metrics—air quality, mobility, mental health—serve as evidence. Architecture favors adaptability over monumentality, embodying humility before change. Public spaces function as epistemic commons where discourse, art, and science meet—the physical manifestation of democratic reason.[20]

9.9 TOWARD THE EUDAIMONIC CIVILIZATION

The ultimate goal of CSR is not intellectual triumph but moral civilization. The Good Society aligns its institutions with the same logic that governs knowledge: test, revise, and improve. It practices

18. Braithwaite, *Crime, Shame and Reintegration*.
19. Farr, *Sustainable Nation*.
20. Habermas, *Between Facts and Norms*.

CHAPTER NINE: THE ARCHITECTURE OF FLOURISHING

fairness through equity, love through compassion, and happiness through harmony with reality.

When truth becomes public, compassion structural, and justice regenerative, humanity enters what may be called the Eudaimonic Civilization—a world that learns ethically.

9.10 MANIFESTO OF THE FLOURISHING WORLD

Let every policy be a hypothesis.
Let every law be tested by life.
Let fairness be our method, compassion our constant,
and truth our measure.

To live well is to live truthfully.
To govern well is to correct mercifully.
To flourish is to align love and reason.

The Splendor of Truth is not above us but among us—
in every warranted act of understanding,
in every kind correction of error,
in every generation that leaves the world more truthful
than it found it.

PART FOUR—ILLUMINATION: THE FULFILLMENT OF KNOWLEDGE

CHAPTER TEN: KNOWLEDGE AND TRANSCENDENCE—THE EPILOGUE OF TRUTH

10.1 INTRODUCTION: THE HORIZON BEYOND KNOWLEDGE

Every philosophy that begins in inquiry must end in wonder. Critical Synthetic Realism (CSR) has led us from the birth of the questioning mind to the architecture of the Good Society; from epistemology to ethics, from logic to love. Yet even as reason refines the world into clarity, a residue of mystery remains. The human mind, no matter how disciplined, confronts a horizon it cannot cross—the horizon of transcendence.

This chapter explores that frontier. It asks: *What lies beyond warranted knowledge?* And more importantly, *how should a rational civilization relate to that which it cannot yet explain?* The answer offered here is not retreat into superstition but reverence through humility—a final synthesis where faith and reason are reconciled through epistemic ethics.

PART FOUR—ILLUMINATION

10.2 THE LIMITS OF THE SYNTHETIC LOOP

The Synthetic Loop—the iterative interaction of Reason, Experience, and Correction—has served throughout this philosophy as the engine of progress.[1] It is humanity's method for converting ignorance into knowledge. But every loop operates within boundaries: the limits of perception, the finitude of time, and the asymptote of complexity.

10.2.1 The Asymptote of Comprehension

Science advances by eliminating error, not by guaranteeing certainty.[2] Each correction extends the boundary of the known, but the infinite totality of truth recedes proportionally. The more we know, the more we realize the vastness of what we do not. CSR calls this the *Asymptote of Comprehension*: the point at which further progress is possible but total completion is impossible. This realization is not despair; it is liberation from arrogance. To know that one cannot know everything is to be freed from the tyranny of dogma.

10.2.2 The Metaphysical Horizon

At the edges of experience stand phenomena that defy current frameworks: consciousness, the origin of existence, the ultimate nature of time. Each generation reframes these mysteries, but none abolish them. The metaphysical horizon functions like the event horizon of a black hole—it conceals what lies beyond, yet its gravitational pull organizes the structure of inquiry. Even ignorance can guide discovery if faced honestly.

---

1. Popper, *Logic of Scientific Discovery*.
2. Kant, *Critique of Pure Reason*.

CHAPTER NINE: THE ARCHITECTURE OF FLOURISHING

10.3 THE ETHICS OF MYSTERY

CSR teaches that truth is absolute, but knowledge is tentative. This gap produces the moral attitude of Epistemic Humility—the recognition that our theories are tools, not thrones.

10.3.1 Faith as Epistemic Humility

Faith, in its most refined sense, is not the negation of reason but the trust that reality is intelligible even when unexplained. When reason reaches its limit, faith functions as the ethical stance that refuses despair or nihilism.[3] It sustains the will to continue inquiry. A scientist's confidence that the universe is lawful, a reformer's conviction that justice is possible, or a parent's belief in their child's potential—these are acts of rational faith, grounded in the unseen but not irrational.

10.3.2 The Moral Dangers of Certitude

The opposite of faith is not doubt but dogmatic certainty. When metaphysical conviction hardens into infallibility—whether in religion, ideology, or nationalism—it becomes destructive. Totalitarian regimes have justified atrocities in the name of final truth.[4] CSR insists that all human belief must remain falsifiable in principle; only the unconditional moral value of truth itself is non-negotiable.

---

3. James, *Varieties of Religious Experience.*
4. Arendt, *Human Condition.*

PART FOUR—ILLUMINATION

10.4 THE CONVERGENCE OF SCIENCE, ART, AND SPIRITUALITY

10.4.1 Science as Reverent Inquiry

Science, at its best, is not a conquest of mystery but an act of reverence toward it. Einstein famously said that "the most beautiful experience we can have is the mysterious." CSR extends this: scientific inquiry is a spiritual practice of disciplined wonder. The astronomer's awe at the cosmos and the monk's awe before the divine share a common emotional grammar—humility before immensity. When science becomes arrogance, it ceases to be science; when religion rejects inquiry, it ceases to be faith. The mature civilization integrates both.

10.4.2 Art as the Bridge of Meaning

If science seeks explanation, art seeks resonance. Art is the aesthetic dimension of truth—the translation of knowledge into felt meaning. A poem, a painting, or a symphony makes the ineffable perceptible without claiming finality.[5] In this sense, art is the sister of philosophy: both strive to unify reason and emotion, fact and value. A civilization that neglects art loses its capacity for empathy—the imaginative rehearsal of possible worlds.

10.4.3 Spirituality as the Ethics of Connection

Spirituality, stripped of dogma, is the awareness of interconnectedness—the felt realization that all agents share the same conditional reality. CSR affirms this in secular terms: every action reverberates through the network of causes and effects. To live spiritually is to act with that awareness, expanding care beyond the self. It is compassion informed by knowledge.

---

5. Nussbaum, *Upheavals of Thought*.

CHAPTER NINE: THE ARCHITECTURE OF FLOURISHING

10.5 THE TRANSCENDENT FUNCTION OF KNOWLEDGE

10.5.1 Knowledge as Participation

The human mind does not merely reflect reality; it participates in its unfolding. Each discovery alters the field of possibility, each moral act reshapes the social fabric. The knowing subject is therefore a co-creator within the conditional cosmos. CSR thus transforms metaphysics into participation: to know is to join the creative rhythm of reality itself.[6]

10.5.2 The Evolution of Consciousness

Knowledge expands not only outward but inward. The evolutionary trajectory of consciousness suggests that as intelligence refines, empathy deepens.[7] The ultimate destiny of the knowing species may not be dominion but communion—a planetary intelligence in which reason and compassion converge. CSR envisions this as the *Noetic Horizon*: the future state in which the world thinks with awareness of its own conditionality.

10.6 DEATH, MEANING, AND THE CONTINUITY OF THE LOOP

10.6.1 Mortality as the Catalyst of Meaning

Death gives urgency to inquiry. The finite lifespan compresses the infinite loop of learning into a human scale, compelling selection and purpose. Every hypothesis we test is provisional, yet its correction echoes beyond us. Mortality transforms the Synthetic Loop

---

6. Dewey, *Quest for Certainty*.
7. Teilhard de Chardin, *Phenomenon of Man*.

PART FOUR—ILLUMINATION

into an intergenerational relay—each mind handing its improved model of reality to the next.[8]

10.6.2 Immortality Through Contribution

The only warranted immortality is epistemic. Ideas, discoveries, and acts of compassion survive their authors by entering the collective knowledge base of humanity. To live well is to add coherence to that corpus. The Good Life, therefore, is not judged by personal comfort but by contribution to the world's accuracy and kindness. The saints of science and justice—Galileo, Curie, King, Mandela—achieved transcendence not through belief in eternity but through their participation in truth.

10.7 THE FUTURE OF REASON—TOWARD AN EPISTEMIC REPUBLIC OF HUMANITY

10.7.1 Global Reason as Moral Imperative

In the political sphere, CSR culminates in the vision of an *Epistemic Republic of Humanity*: a global order grounded in fairness, transparency, and warranted cooperation. Just as democracy institutionalizes falsifiability within nations, global governance must institutionalize it among nations.[9] International law, climate accords, and digital ethics all require continuous correction through shared evidence. Nationalism must yield to epistemic patriotism—the loyalty to truth above tribe.

---

8. Heidegger, *Being and Time*.
9. Habermas, *Between Facts and Norms*.

10.7.2 Technology as the New Frontier of Moral Evolution

Artificial intelligence, genetic engineering, and planetary management technologies confront us with godlike powers absent godlike wisdom. CSR provides the ethical compass: every invention must be evaluated by its coherence with conditional reality and its contribution to human flourishing.[10] The measure of progress is not speed or novelty but the reduction of ignorance and suffering.

10.8 THE SPLENDOR OF TRUTH—FINAL REFLECTIONS

All along this philosophical journey, we have sought the meaning of truth not as possession but as relationship. Truth is not a static object; it is the living correspondence between intellect and reality, between love and justice. The Splendor of Truth is this radiant equilibrium—the light produced when mind and world meet without distortion.

To live truthfully is therefore to live beautifully. The moral task of civilization is to preserve this beauty: to keep inquiry honest, compassion vivid, and institutions corrigible. In doing so, humanity becomes the consciousness of the cosmos—a self-correcting witness to its own becoming.

---

10. Bostrom, *Superintelligence*.

PART FOUR—ILLUMINATION

10.9 BENEDICTION: THE PRAYER OF THE RATIONAL HEART

Let knowledge remain humble,
and wonder remain bold.
Let every question be asked in love,
and every answer serve compassion.

May our science never silence our awe,
nor our faith forbid our doubt.

For the world is not finished,
and neither are we.

The Splendor of Truth shines not in certainty,
but in the ever-unfolding dialogue
between what is known
and what is yet to be understood.

Epilogue: Truth as Liberation—The Final Victory of Knowledge

We have journeyed through the realms of conditional reality, established the nature of provisional knowledge, and translated epistemic responsibility into a comprehensive architecture for the individual and society. We started with the humble recognition of the Epistemic Barrier—that separation between what we truly know and what we merely wish to believe—and ended by defining Eudaimonia as the flourishing found in the alignment of mind and reality.

Now, we come to the end of the inquiry, only to realize that the end of the inquiry is the beginning of action. The entire project of Critical Synthetic Realism (CSR) is, at its core, a simple declaration: Truth is Liberation.

Moral freedom is often mistaken for the license to act without consequence. But true, *warranted* freedom is the capacity to choose and act effectively within the bounds of conditional causality. This capacity is born not of sentiment or wishful thinking, but of rigorous knowledge. The agent who understands reality's constraints—who accepts that all results are conditional upon warranted effort—is the only agent truly free, because they are

EPILOGUE: TRUTH AS LIBERATION

the only one whose effort is systematically guaranteed to yield predictable, defensible progress.

The liberation promised by truth is three-fold:

11.1 RESISTANCE AGAINST IGNORANCE (THE INTERNAL TYRANT)

The greatest oppressor we face is not external but internal: Ignorance. Ignorance binds us to the Causal Fallacy, convincing us that our intentions alone determine results, or that immutable forces beyond our control dictate our fate. This delusion destroys Agency by denying us the ability to recognize our own leverage points.

The search for truth is the highest form of resistance to this tyranny. When the agent embraces the Synthetic Loop—the continuous process of hypothesis, testing, and correction—they free themselves from the mental slavery of delusion. To commit to warranted knowledge is to declare intellectual sovereignty over your own experience. It is the refusal to suspend judgment, the refusal to believe what is comforting instead of what is testable, and the ultimate act of Epistemic Responsibility.

11.2 RESISTANCE AGAINST FEAR (THE EMOTIONAL CAGE)

Fear is merely the emotional manifestation of ignorance. We fear what we do not understand, or what we believe is arbitrary and uncontrollable. The agent operating in darkness fears the consequence of every step.

By illuminating the world with critically pursued knowledge, we replace the panic of the arbitrary with the calm of the conditional. When we understand the *conditions* of failure, we lose the *fear* of failure. We realize that failure is not a personal indictment but merely a data point, an expected and necessary input for the next, more successful iteration.

EPILOGUE: TRUTH AS LIBERATION

Truth disarms fear by making reality predictable. The liberated mind accepts provisionality, knowing that while certainty is impossible, warranted clarity is achievable, offering a profound sense of psychological peace—the very essence of Happiness.

11.3 RESISTANCE AGAINST OPPRESSION (THE SOCIAL CONSTRUCT)

Oppression, whether political, economic, or social, is always predicated on the systematic imposition of an unwarranted reality upon the oppressed. Tyrannies thrive by censoring data, demanding irrational belief, and isolating agents from their capacity for self-correction.

The pursuit of truth, therefore, is the engine of Democracy. The collective commitment to the Integrity Rule—to speak the warranted data, to provide warranted critique, and to defend the Agency of every other participant—is the only structure that can withstand the perpetual pressure of tyranny and corruption. Our insistence on Fairness and Equity is simply the political application of the rule that all agents must have the necessary access to perform their warranted work.

The ultimate moral conviction of this philosophy is that humanity possesses the inherent, conditional capacity to solve its greatest problems—to heal its wounds, reverse its ecological damage, and build structures of justice and kindness. This capacity is called Global Agency.

This agency is not a future utopian gift; it is a current responsibility. It is achieved not through magical thinking, but through the rigorous, collective application of warranted knowledge. The search for truth—critical, synthetic, and ceaseless—is the light we must all carry. By this light, and by this light alone, humanity will achieve its full, liberated potential.

Postscript: In the Light of the Unfinished

I have spent much of my life chasing truth through the shifting corridors of faith and reason. The seminaries taught me reverence; the universities taught me skepticism; the world itself—broken, beautiful, and unfinished—taught me the humility of uncertainty.

Somewhere along that long road from doctrine to discovery, I began to understand that truth is not a possession but a pilgrimage. It is not found in creeds or formulas, but in the quiet courage to ask again—especially when the answers we inherited no longer suffice.

Critical Synthetic Realism was born not in a laboratory or a monastery, but in the tension between the two—the need to reconcile devotion with doubt, certainty with compassion. It became, for me, a way of living: a discipline of seeing clearly, correcting gently, and believing boldly that reason itself is sacred when it serves love.

I have come to believe that God, if the word still means anything, is not the author of fixed certainties but the living horizon of intelligibility—the source of order that invites, not commands, our participation. Faith, then, is not submission to mystery, but cooperation with it. It is the refusal to abandon the work of understanding simply because the work is endless.

POSTSCRIPT: IN THE LIGHT OF THE UNFINISHED

Throughout these pages, I have tried to honor the intellect as a moral faculty, to show that the search for knowledge is also the search for goodness. Yet I end not as a philosopher triumphant, but as a pilgrim still in motion. I know now that the mind's last act of wisdom is gratitude—to thank the world for being both knowable and beyond our knowing, to thank the countless teachers, friends, and students whose questions sharpened my own, and to thank the invisible grace that keeps wonder alive in an age of cynicism.

If this work has a single prayer, it is that humanity might learn to see truth not as a sword to divide, but as a light to share. May we build schools and nations that reward honesty, cultivate compassion, and refuse to make peace with ignorance. May we learn to disagree without hatred, to doubt without despair, and to love without illusion.

For in the end, all philosophy becomes autobiography: every argument a reflection of the heart that uttered it. My own journey—across faiths, disciplines, and continents—has convinced me that the deepest vocation of the thinker is not to be right, but to be real: to live in such fidelity to truth that even one's errors become part of its unfolding.

So I close, not with a conclusion, but with a confession:
|I remain a believer—
in reason as grace,
in love as knowledge,
and in truth as the most demanding, most liberating prayer
the human spirit can ever utter.

Appendix I: The Conceptual Model of Critical Synthetic Realism (CSR)

This document outlines the core structural components and operational flow of the Critical Synthetic Realism (CSR) Framework, defining the relationship between reality, knowledge, and ethical action.

I. CORE AXIOMS

The entire framework rests on two non-negotiable axioms:

Axiom	Definition	Implication for Agency
1. Conditional Reality	All outcomes—physical, psychological, social, and economic—are conditional upon specific, identifiable antecedent inputs (causes). No result is guaranteed or arbitrary.	Agency is conditional. The individual's power is limited by the rules of reality, but maximized by the knowledge of those rules.
2. Epistemic Responsibility	The moral duty of every agent to continuously test, correct, and upgrade their beliefs and models of reality based on the best available, corroborated data.	Moral duty is tied to knowledge. To act without rigorous knowledge is to risk causing unnecessary harm, making it an ethical failure.

APPENDIX I: THE CONCEPTUAL MODEL OF CSR

II. THE CORE CONCEPTS OF CSR

The following table defines the essential vocabulary used in the framework, moving from fundamental problems to desired outcomes.

Concept	Definition	Function/Role
Epistemic Barrier	The inherent, often protected gap between subjective belief (what one *wants* to be true) and objective, testable reality (what *is* true).	The fundamental challenge to be overcome by the agent.
The Causal Fallacy	The primary error state: the mistaken belief that intention, wishful thinking, or sentiment alone dictates results, ignoring conditional causality.	The source of Ignorance and ineffective action.
Synthetic Loop	The operational, continuous feedback cycle of hypothesis, testing, data synthesis, and correction, designed to generate Warranted Knowledge.	The mechanism for bridging the Epistemic Barrier.
Warranted Knowledge	A belief or model that has survived rigorous testing against Conditional Reality and offers the highest predictive validity for a conditional outcome.	The output of the Synthetic Loop and the basis for action.
Warranted Effort	Action taken based on Warranted Knowledge; effort that has a predictable, evidence-backed probability of achieving a desired, conditional outcome.	The only form of effort that guarantees progress.
Agency	The individual's power to choose and act effectively. It is derived from understanding and successfully applying Conditional Causality.	The goal of individual growth and freedom.

APPENDIX I: THE CONCEPTUAL MODEL OF CSR

Concept	Definition	Function/Role
Integrity Rule	The collective commitment within a social system (democracy, team, market) to provide and defend honest, warranted critique and data.	The foundation of ethical, functional social and political structures.
Global Agency	The collective, conditional capacity of humanity to solve global problems (e.g., climate, injustice) through the unified application of Warranted Knowledge.	The ultimate ethical and political ambition of the framework.
Eudaimonia	Human flourishing achieved through the active, continuous alignment of the mind (beliefs) with Conditional Reality.	The ultimate philosophical goal (The highest form of Happiness).

III. THE SYNTHETIC LOOP

The Synthetic Loop is the engine of CSR. A visual representation of this loop would demonstrate the continuous, recursive nature of knowledge generation.

The diagram illustrates the flow required to convert a mere hypothesis into Warranted Knowledge, which in turn fuels effective action.

The Four Stages of the Synthetic Loop:

1. Hypothesis (Prediction): An agent forms an explicit, testable prediction about a conditional outcome in reality (e.g., "If I apply Method X, I will achieve Result Y"). This is based on current, provisional knowledge.
2. Testing (Effort/Action): The agent takes Warranted Effort based on the Hypothesis. They execute the necessary actions and collect raw data on the outcome.

APPENDIX I: THE CONCEPTUAL MODEL OF CSR

3. Data Synthesis (Critique): The agent critically compares the actual results (the collected data) against the initial Hypothesis (the prediction).
4. Correction (Upgrade/Discard):
    - If the result matches the prediction, the current model is upgraded to a higher level of Warranted Knowledge.
    - If the result fails to match, the model is corrected or discarded, and the cycle returns to Stage 1 with a new, better-informed Hypothesis.

This loop must be *continuous* because, under Conditional Reality, no knowledge is final, only provisional. The commitment to this loop is the essence of Epistemic Responsibility.

Appendix II: Glossary of Key Terms

A

Agency (Epistemic and Moral)

The capacity of the rational agent to act upon reality through warranted knowledge. In CSR, agency is conditional—it expands with understanding and contracts with ignorance. True freedom is not the absence of limits but the mastery of conditions.

Axiological Distinction

The separation between the *value* of a belief or action (its emotional, cultural, or moral worth) and its *epistemic warrant* (its factual validity). This distinction allows CSR to affirm the psychological benefits of faith or prayer without granting them causal efficacy in the material world.

B

Belief (Warranted vs. Unwarranted)

A cognitive commitment to a proposition. Warranted belief is grounded in Reason, Experience, Coherence, and Testimony—the four sources of justified knowledge. Unwarranted belief, by contrast, relies on authority, intuition, or comfort without verification.

APPENDIX II: GLOSSARY OF KEY TERMS

C

Causal Fallacy

The mistaken assumption that outcomes can be achieved without satisfying the conditional causes that make them possible (e.g., success without effort, healing without treatment). It is the central error CSR seeks to correct.

Coherence (Criterion of Truth)

A standard of justification whereby a belief is considered true if it fits logically and consistently within a wider network of already warranted beliefs. Coherence ensures internal consistency, though it must be complemented by Correspondence to external reality.

Conditional Causality

The principle that every effect arises from a set of necessary and sufficient conditions that can, in principle, be identified, tested, and reproduced. In CSR, this principle grounds both science and ethics—effort must match cause.

Critical Synthetic Realism (CSR)

The central philosophical framework of this book. CSR posits that truth is both knowable and provisional, grounded in the dynamic interaction between Reason, Experience, Coherence, and Testimony—all tested by Criticality (falsifiability and ethical scrutiny). It is "Critical" because it subjects all claims to error-checking, "Synthetic" because it unifies diverse modes of knowing, and "Realist" because it affirms an objective world independent of the mind.

Criticality (Epistemic and Ethical)

The methodological and moral obligation to question, test, and potentially falsify every claim to truth. Criticality protects the knowledge system from dogma, ideology, and power-based distortion.

APPENDIX II: GLOSSARY OF KEY TERMS

Correspondence (Criterion of Truth)

The test of truth as *adequatio intellectus et rei*—the agreement between intellect and reality. A proposition is true if what it asserts corresponds to what objectively exists.

D

Democracy (Epistemic Democracy)

The political institutionalization of the Synthetic Loop. It translates the logic of scientific falsification into public governance: policy as hypothesis, experience as test, and elections as correction. Democracy is, for CSR, reason made social.

Destiny (Fatalism)

The unwarranted belief that life's outcomes are fixed by supernatural decree. CSR rejects fatalism as an epistemic abdication, affirming instead that human progress depends on conditional causality and the moral duty of effort.

E

Epistemic Humility

The awareness that truth is absolute, but our knowledge of it is always provisional. It is the moral attitude that replaces arrogance with continuous learning.

Epistemic Responsibility

The ethical duty to ensure that one's beliefs and actions are grounded in warranted knowledge. It is the virtue that links truth-seeking with justice.

Epistemic Sovereignty

The capacity of a community or nation to generate, verify, and act upon its own warranted knowledge, free from ideological or external control. A precondition for true political and economic independence.

APPENDIX II: GLOSSARY OF KEY TERMS

Epistemic Fracture

The collapse of a culture's Synthetic Loop—when inquiry gives way to dogma and institutions stop self-correcting. In CSR, this is the root cause of underdevelopment, corruption, and intellectual stagnation.

Epistemic Loop (or Synthetic Loop)

The continuous cycle of hypothesis (Reason), testing (Experience), coherence-checking, and correction (Criticality). This is the epistemological heartbeat of CSR and the mechanism of all genuine progress.

F

Fairness (Conditional Justice)

The ethical recognition that outcomes should be proportionate to warranted effort. A fair society ensures access to necessary inputs (education, health, liberty) while holding individuals accountable for the conditional consequences of their actions.

Faith (Rational Faith)

An existential posture of trust in the intelligibility of reality and the meaningfulness of inquiry. Unlike dogmatic faith, rational faith does not oppose evidence but inspires the courage to seek it.

Freedom (Warranted Freedom)

The capacity to act effectively within the constraints of reality. CSR defines freedom not as the absence of limits but as the informed use of them—the art of making conditional choices that yield predictable, moral outcomes.

G

Global Agency

Humanity's collective capacity to act intelligently and cooperatively on a planetary scale through the application of warranted knowledge. The highest political and moral horizon of CSR.

Good Life (Eudaimonia)

The flourishing state achieved when Truth (knowledge), Freedom (agency), and Virtue (epistemic responsibility) converge. It is the psychological peace and moral joy of a life aligned with reality.

H

Happiness (Epistemic Peace)

Not mere pleasure but the tranquility of a mind in harmony with truth. The emotional dividend of a warranted worldview.

Humility (Epistemic)

The recognition that correction is more valuable than pride—that the willingness to revise one's belief is the highest form of wisdom.

I

Integrity Rule

The ethical law that demands coherence between word, thought, and fact. Public lies, corruption, and manipulation are violations of the Integrity Rule, as they replace warranted testimony with deliberate falsehood.

Illusion of Omniscience

The false sense of completeness created by modern AI and media systems, where algorithmic coherence is mistaken for truth. CSR insists that coherence without correspondence produces delusion.

APPENDIX II: GLOSSARY OF KEY TERMS

K

Knowledge (Warranted Knowledge)

Information that has passed the full Synthetic Loop—justified through reason, verified by experience, consistent with prior truths, and open to correction. Knowledge is power only when it is warranted; otherwise, it is manipulation.

L

Love (Warranted Love)

The rational and compassionate commitment to the flourishing of another agent. True love respects the other's conditional nature, balancing compassion (grace) with justice (truth).

M

Miracle (Epistemically Unwarrantable Event)

An event claimed to violate conditional causality. CSR does not deny the possibility of transcendence but asserts that no causal claim can be warranted without conditional explanation.

Misinformation (Epistemic Corruption)

The deliberate or negligent propagation of unwarranted claims that distort public understanding and disable the collective Synthetic Loop.

P

Prayer (Therapeutic vs. Mechanistic)

In CSR, prayer has value as *Therapy* (psychological coherence, emotional regulation) but not as *Mechanism* (direct alteration of material reality without conditional work).

APPENDIX II: GLOSSARY OF KEY TERMS

Provisionality

The state of being open to revision. In CSR, provisionality is not weakness but the sign of strength—the permanent readiness to learn.

R

Realism (Metaphysical)

The affirmation that a reality exists independently of perception, belief, or desire. Truth is correspondence to that reality, not consensus about it.

Reason (A Priori Structure)

The rational faculty that generates hypotheses and logical order. In CSR, reason is both a creative and corrective power—one half of the Synthetic Loop.

S

Sustainability (Intergenerational Fairness)

The moral and practical commitment to ensure that present flourishing does not destroy the conditions for future flourishing. Sustainability extends conditional causality across time.

Synthetic Loop (Cycle of Warrant)

The recursive, self-correcting process through which knowledge evolves: Reason → Experience → Coherence → Correction. The model of both science and morality in CSR.

T

Testimony (Social Knowledge)

Validated, transmitted knowledge from credible sources. Testimony allows civilization to accumulate progress but must be constantly checked for integrity.

APPENDIX II: GLOSSARY OF KEY TERMS

Truth (Aletheia / Adaequatio)

The alignment between intellect and reality (*adaequatio intellectus et rei*). In CSR, truth is objective but only knowable through continuous testing and correction. Truth liberates because it reveals the conditions of agency.

Truth as Liberation

The ultimate moral claim of CSR: knowledge frees the mind from ignorance, fear, and domination, restoring both individual and collective agency.

Utility vs. Truth

Utility measures usefulness; truth measures correspondence. The two may overlap, but CSR insists that utility without truth is manipulation, and truth without compassion is cruelty.

W

Warrant

The degree of justified confidence that a claim reflects reality. A claim achieves warrant only when it passes the fourfold test of CSR: Reason, Experience, Coherence, and Testimony.

Work (Conditional Effort)

The ethical act of aligning intention with causal necessity. In CSR, "To work is to pray"—effort is the only warranted mechanism of transformation in the material world.

Z

Zenith of Knowledge (The Splendor of Truth)

The final moral and intellectual goal of CSR: the luminous condition in which the human spirit and the structure of reality converge in understanding. The Splendor of Truth is not revelation but illumination—the peace of living consciously within the light of reason.

Appendix III: The CSR Method in Education and Policy—Practical Applications

The power of Critical Synthetic Realism (CSR) lies in its ability to take abstract philosophical principles (Conditional Reality and Epistemic Responsibility) and translate them into operational, testable methodologies for improving human systems.

I. APPLICATION IN EDUCATION: THE WARRANTED KNOWLEDGE CURRICULUM

CSR views education not as the transmission of facts, but as the process of training Agency—the capacity to effectively generate and use Warranted Knowledge.

The Problem CSR Solves in Education

The traditional model often reinforces the Epistemic Barrier by rewarding students who can memorize and repeat information provided by an authority (the teacher or textbook). This practice

APPENDIX III: THE CSR METHOD IN EDUCATION AND POLICY

teaches unwarranted belief and reinforces the Causal Fallacy (believing a grade is conditional on effort alone, rather than effort *applied effectively*).

The CSR Educational Method: Teaching the Synthetic Loop

The goal is to shift the educational focus from *content* mastery to *process* mastery. Students learn that all knowledge is provisional and must be earned through the Synthetic Loop (Hypothesis, Testing, Critique, Correction).

Component	Traditional Approach	CSR Application (Warranted Knowledge Curriculum)
Learning Objective	To recall information (e.g., memorize historical dates).	To design a verifiable method (e.g., predict the outcome of a social policy given specific variables).
Assessment	Examinations that test memorization.	Warranted Project Review: Grades are weighted heavily on the rigor of the Synthetic Loop used, not just the final result. Was the hypothesis testable? Was the data sufficient? Was the critique honest?
Failure	A final, negative judgment that destroys motivation.	Data Synthesis Input: Failure is rebranded as the most valuable data point, proving that the model (hypothesis) was conditional upon variables missed. It triggers the immediate return to the Correction stage.
Teacher's Role	Authority and information provider.	Epistemic Guide: Facilitates the Testing phase and mandates the use of the Integrity Rule in peer review (demanding honest critique).

APPENDIX III: THE CSR METHOD IN EDUCATION AND POLICY

Outcome: Students develop Epistemic Humility, knowing that they are always wrong *until proven right*, and possess Agency because they know *how* to become more right.

II. APPLICATION IN POLICY AND GOVERNANCE: CONDITIONAL POLICY ARCHITECTURE

In policy, the principles of CSR ensure that governance is adaptive, self-correcting, and aligned with measurable reality, rather than fixed ideology.

The Problem CSR Solves in Policy

Policies often fail due to the Causal Fallacy on a grand scale: a government or institution implements a policy because it *feels* right, *sounds* moral, or is dictated by ideology, rather than because it has survived rigorous, warranted testing. This leads to path dependency—continuing a failing policy due to political cost or institutional inertia.

The CSR Governance Method: Operationalizing Conditional Reality

Policy development must be structured as a continuous, massive-scale Synthetic Loop, where every piece of legislation is treated as a high-stakes Hypothesis about a future conditional outcome.

1. Conditional Policy Design (The Hypothesis Phase)

   Every proposed policy must explicitly state its Conditional Outcome in measurable terms.

   - Mandatory Component: All legislation must include a Metric of Failure.
     - *Example*: A job training policy cannot just state "will improve job prospects." It must state: "If

unemployment in Target Demographic A has not decreased by 4% within 36 months, the policy is legally defined as failed and must enter the Critique phase."

2. Enforcement of the Integrity Rule (The Testing Phase)

The governing body must legally protect the mechanisms of Critique and data collection.

- Audit Function: Independent, non-political agencies are mandated to collect and publish data, regardless of whether it supports or contradicts the governing party's desired outcome.

- Warranted Debate: Political debate shifts from emotional persuasion to a competition of Warranted Knowledge—arguments must be backed by transparent, peer-reviewed data and testable models.

3. Structured Correction (The Synthesis and Correction Phase)

When the Metric of Failure is met, the policy automatically triggers a mandated phase of Correction.

- The legislature is legally required to move immediately into a Data Synthesis session, where the only objective is to analyze *why* the conditions for success were not met.

- The original policy is not merely repealed; it is corrected—the new version must incorporate the failure data, refine the variables, and establish a new, testable Hypothesis.

Outcome: A system of Adaptive Governance where policy is never static and is constantly correcting toward Global Agency—the collective capacity to achieve measurable, just outcomes for all citizens.

ABOUT THE AUTHOR

Dr. Januarius Jingwa (JJ) Asongu is an American philosopher, liberation theologian, cybersecurity executive, educator, and prolific author whose interdisciplinary achievements span philosophy, theology, psychology, journalism, information technology, business administration, risk governance, and higher-education leadership. Renowned for his intellectual breadth, moral clarity, and commitment to human dignity, he stands as a compelling voice at the intersection of thought, technology, spirituality, and social justice.

Born on August 17, 1970, in Lewoh, Lebialem, he was raised in a Catholic family that valued discipline, faith, education, and service. As a student leader in the Young Christian Students (YCS) movement at Government High School Kumbo (now GBHS Kumbo), he facilitated discussions on ethics, justice, leadership, and social transformation. These early experiences shaped his worldview and anchored his lifelong commitment to liberating the human person from political, religious, and institutional oppression.

Dr. Asongu pursued formal philosophical and theological formation at St. Thomas Aquinas Major Seminary (STAMS) in Bambui, earning the Bachelor of Philosophy (BPhil) degree in 1993 through the Pontifical Urban University in Rome. His seminary studies immersed him in metaphysics, epistemology, classical philosophy, scholasticism, logic, ethics, and systematic theology. He

ABOUT THE AUTHOR

also earned certificates in Latin and Biblical Greek, enriching his engagement with classical Christian texts and the linguistic foundations of Catholic intellectual tradition.

His intellectual identity was profoundly shaped by the liberative theological and philosophical thinkers he encountered during these years. Gustavo Gutiérrez, Leonardo Boff, Paulo Freire, and Jean-Marc Éla inspired in him a theology rooted in justice, liberation, and solidarity with the oppressed. John Henry Newman's insights on conscience and the development of doctrine, Bernard Häring's moral theology, Karl Rahner's transcendental theology, Hans Küng's ecumenism, Karl Popper's critical rationalism, and the pioneering works of African scholars Bernard Fonlon and Bongasu Tanla-Kishani further shaped his conviction that truth must transcend institutional boundaries and that scholarship must contribute to human emancipation. He was also deeply influenced by Frantz Fanon—especially *The Wretched of the Earth*—whose revolutionary psychological and political analysis sharpened his understanding of structural violence, dehumanization, and the urgent necessity of liberation-centered praxis.

Complementing these influences were two philosophical pillars that continue to guide his life's work. First, St. Anselm's classic formulation of theology as *"faith seeking understanding"* (fides quaerens intellectum), which affirmed for him that authentic faith welcomes inquiry, reason, and intellectual humility. Second, the classical Greek concept of eudaimonia, the vision of human flourishing through virtue, wisdom, and purposeful living. These frameworks helped shape his understanding of education, leadership, and service as pathways toward the full development of the human person.

After seminary, Dr. Asongu expanded his intellectual and professional pursuits into journalism and public communication. He earned a Certificate in Journalism from the University of Lagos in 1995 and completed a Wolfson Press Fellowship at the University of Cambridge in 1998. That same year, he completed a PhD in

ABOUT THE AUTHOR

Communication from Pacific Western University (now California Miramar University). He later distinguished himself as an Alfred Friendly Press Fellow at *The Houston Chronicle*, where he contributed analyses on global affairs, politics, and social ethics. Across his career, he has published numerous articles in academic journals and the public press, enriching public discourse on theology, governance, ethics, psychology, and technology.

In 2002, he earned a Master of Science in Information Technology from the University of Maryland University College (UMGC). He began doctoral studies in Business Administration at Argosy University, then transferred to Charisma University, where he completed his PhD in Business Administration in 2011 and another in Cybersecurity Administration in 2015. In 2025, he completed a PhD in Psychology from City University of Cambodia, adding human behavior, cognitive science, and mental health to his intellectual repertoire.

Over the last decade, Dr. Asongu has cultivated a distinguished career in cybersecurity, IT governance, and enterprise risk. He has served at the U.S. Department of Homeland Security (Science & Technology Directorate), Citi, City National Bank, JPMorgan Chase, Boston Consulting Group (BCG), SMBC Group, Ernst & Young, Truist, Coinbase, Kyndryl, Freddie Mac, Fannie Mae, IBM, and the U.S. Department of Defense. His expertise encompasses NIST RMF and CSF, ISO 27001, SOX, GLBA, cloud security, operational resilience, identity governance, cybersecurity strategy, third-party risk management, and emerging-technology oversight.

He holds more than a dozen elite professional certifications—including CCIO, CISA, CISM, CRISC, CDPSE, CGEIT, CISSP, AWS Security Specialty, ITIL, PMP, Scrum Master Certified, CPP, IBM Blockchain Essentials, and Google AI Essentials—placing him among the most extensively credentialed cybersecurity and governance professionals in the field.

ABOUT THE AUTHOR

In parallel, he has enjoyed a dynamic academic career, teaching at over a dozen universities. He rose to the rank of Associate Professor at Herzing University and has also taught at Rockford University, Fort Hays State University, Franklin University, and Embry-Riddle Aeronautical University, among others. He has supervised numerous graduate research projects, including a PhD dissertation at the prestigious University of Paris, Sorbonne.

In 2012, Dr. Asongu founded Saint Monica University (SMU), an American-style liberal arts and technology university with operations in Cameroon and Sierra Leone. As Chancellor, he champions an educational philosophy at the intersection of liberal arts and technology, rooted in critical thinking, ethical leadership, global citizenship, innovation, justice, and community transformation.

He is the author of an extensive body of published work. His solo-authored books include:

1. *The Graduate Research Companion: A Step-by-Step Handbook for Thesis Writers*
2. *Cybersecurity & Emerging Technologies: A Pocket Dictionary for Students and Professionals*
3. *Forced Unity: A Critical Appraisal of the Ambazonia Struggle for Emancipation and Self-Determination*
4. *Hidden Selves: Triple Masking and the Mental Health Crisis in the Church*
5. *Holistic Resilience: Counseling at the Intersection of Faith, Family, and Identity*
6. *Strategic Corporate Social Responsibility in Practice*
7. *War, Politics and Business: A Critique of the Global War on Terror*

His co-authored works include:

1. *Industrial Engineering Essentials: A Degree-Completion Guide* (with Wilson Taza)

ABOUT THE AUTHOR

2. *Advanced Microbiology and Parasitology* (with Elijah T. Daniel)

3. *Educational Psychology: Integrating Global Learning Sciences with African Educational Realities* (with Nicholas Asongu Jingwa)

4. *Global Logistics & Supply Chain Management* (with Daryl-Palma Asongu Nguatem)

5. *Unpacking the Mind* (with George Alberto Gonzalez)

6. *Doing Business Abroad* (with C'Lamt Ho and Marvee Marr)

7. *The Iraq Quagmire* (with Stephen Lendman)

8. *Technology in Education and Business: Myths, Issues, Ethics, and Money* (with Dana Lundell)

Throughout his work, Dr. Asongu is guided by Anselm's "faith seeking understanding," Newman's conscience and doctrinal development, the classical ideal of eudaimonia, and—above all—the critical rationalism of Karl Popper, whose influence surpasses that of all other thinkers in shaping his commitment to openness, inquiry, and the progressive, self-correcting nature of knowledge. These frameworks ground his belief that the pursuit of truth is inseparable from the pursuit of human flourishing.

At his core, Dr. Asongu remains a philosopher devoted to truth, justice, conscience, and the flourishing of humanity. Across his writing, teaching, leadership, and service, his life bears witness to one animating conviction: the purpose of knowledge is liberation, and the purpose of leadership is the flourishing of the human person and society.

Dr. Asongu resides in Townsend, Delaware, with his wife Christine Ngangsic and their children Jude, Maria, and Bernard. His family remains the living center of his philosophy—a daily practice of fairness, love, and intellectual humility.

Whether teaching, writing, or reflecting, Dr. Asongu continues to embody a rare synthesis of intellect, compassion, and vision. His life

ABOUT THE AUTHOR

stands as an argument for the possibility of unity amid diversity: the unity of reason and revelation, Africa and America, faith and freedom. He belongs to that enduring lineage of thinkers who remind the world that truth is not merely to be known—it is to be lived.

BIBLIOGRAPHY

Acton, John Emerich Edward Dalberg. "Letter to Bishop Mandell Creighton." In *Historical Essays and Studies*, edited by J. N. Figgis and R. V. Laurence, 504–506. London: Macmillan, 1887.
Adogame, Afe. *The African Christian Diaspora: New Currents and Emerging Trends in World Christianity*. London: Bloomsbury, 2013.
Ammerman, Nancy T. *Sacred Stories, Spiritual Tribes: Finding Religion in Everyday Life*. Oxford: Oxford University Press, 2014.
Amnesty International. *Cameroon: A Turn for the Worse—Violence and Human Rights Violations in Anglophone Cameroon*. London: Amnesty International Publications, 2018.
Archer, Margaret S. *Realist Social Theory: The Morphogenetic Approach*. Cambridge: Cambridge University Press, 1995.
Arendt, Hannah. *The Human Condition*. Chicago: University of Chicago Press, 1958.
Asongu, Januarius J. *Cybersecurity & Emerging Technologies: A Pocket Dictionary for Students and Professionals*. Townsend, DE: Saint Monica University Press, 2025.
———. *Cybersecurity Governance, Risk, and Compliance: Foundations for Secure and Resilient Organizations*. Townsend, DE: Saint Monica University Press, 2025.
———. *Forced Unity: A Critical Appraisal of the Ambazonia Struggle for Emancipation and Self-Determination*. Townsend, DE: Saint Monica University Press, 2025.
———. *Hidden Selves: Triple Masking and the Mental Health Crisis in the Church*. Townsend, DE: Saint Monica University Press, 2025.
———. *Holistic Resilience: Counseling at the Intersection of Faith, Family, and Identity*. Townsend, DE: Saint Monica University Press, 2025.
———. *Strategic Corporate Social Responsibility in Practice*. Lawrenceville, GA: Greenview, 2007.

BIBLIOGRAPHY

———. *Strategic Corporate Social Responsibility in Practice: Institutions, Strategy, Innovation, Marketing, and Global Legitimacy.* 2nd ed. Townsend, DE: Saint Monica University Press, 2025.

———. *The Graduate Research Companion: A Step-by-Step Handbook for Thesis Writers.* Townsend, DE: Saint Monica University Press, 2025.

———. *The Human Firewall: How Organizational Culture Shapes Cybersecurity Behavior.* Townsend, DE: Saint Monica University Press, 2025.

———. *The Modern MBA: Core Concepts and Strategies for Global Business Leaders.* Townsend, DE: Saint Monica University Press, 2025.

———. *Technology in Education and Business: Myths, Issues, Ethics, and Money.* Lawrenceville, GA: Greenview, 2007.

———. *War, Politics and Business: A Critique of the Global War on Terror.* Lawrenceville, GA: Greenview, 2007.

Asongu, Januarius J., and Elijah T. Daniel. *Advanced Microbiology and Parasitology.* Townsend, DE: Saint Monica University Press, 2025.

Asongu, Januarius J., and George Alberto Gonzalez. *Unpacking the Mind.* Townsend, DE: Saint Monica University Press, 2025.

Asongu, Januarius J., and Nicholas Asongu Jingwa. *Educational Psychology: Integrating Global Learning Sciences with African Educational Realities.* Townsend, DE: Saint Monica University Press, 2025.

Asongu, Januarius J., and Daryl-Palma Asongu Nguatem. *Global Logistics & Supply Chain Management.* Townsend, DE: Saint Monica University Press, 2025.

Asongu, Januarius J., C'Lamt Ho, and Marvee Marr. *Doing Business Abroad.* Lawrenceville, GA: Greenview, 2007.

Asongu, Januarius J., and Dana Lundell, eds. *Technology in Education and Business: Myths, Issues, Ethics, and Money.* Lawrenceville, GA: Greenview, 2007.

Asongu, Januarius J., and Wilson Taza. *Industrial Engineering Essentials: A Degree-Completion Guide.* Townsend, DE: Saint Monica University Press, 2025.

Aswân, Salah, Fred Wendorf, and Romuald Schild. *The Geology and Archaeology of the Western Desert of Egypt.* Dallas: Southern Methodist University Press, 2005.

Becker, Ernest. *The Denial of Death.* New York: Free Press, 1973.

Berlin, Isaiah. *Two Concepts of Liberty.* Oxford: Clarendon Press, 1969.

Berger, Peter L., ed. *The Desecularization of the World: Resurgent Religion and World Politics.* Grand Rapids, MI: Eerdmans, 1999.

Bhaskar, Roy. *A Realist Theory of Science.* Brighton: Harvester Press, 1978.

Bowler, Kate. *Blessed: A History of the American Prosperity Gospel.* New York: Oxford University Press, 2013.

Brown, Wendy. *Undoing the Demos: Neoliberalism's Stealth Revolution.* New York: Zone Books, 2015.

Bruce, Steve. *Secularization: In Defence of an Unfashionable Theory.* Oxford: Oxford University Press, 2011.

BIBLIOGRAPHY

Buber, Martin. *I and Thou*. Translated by Ronald Gregor Smith. New York: Charles Scribner's Sons, 1958.

Campbell, Heidi A. *Digital Religion: Understanding Religious Practice in New Media Worlds*. London: Routledge, 2013.

Carrette, Jeremy, and Richard King. *Selling Spirituality: The Silent Takeover of Religion*. London: Routledge, 2005.

Casanova, José. *Public Religions in the Modern World*. Chicago: University of Chicago Press, 1994.

Coleman, Simon. *The Globalisation of Charismatic Christianity: Spreading the Gospel of Prosperity*. Cambridge: Cambridge University Press, 2000.

Comaroff, Jean, and John L. Comaroff. *Ethnicity, Inc.* Chicago: University of Chicago Press, 2009.

Csikszentmihalyi, Mihaly. *Flow: The Psychology of Optimal Experience*. New York: Harper & Row, 1990.

Damasio, Antonio. *The Feeling of What Happens: Body and Emotion in the Making of Consciousness*. New York: Harcourt Brace, 1999.

Denzin, Norman K., and Yvonna S. Lincoln, eds. *The SAGE Handbook of Qualitative Research*. 5th ed. Thousand Oaks, CA: SAGE, 2018.

Dewey, John. *Democracy and Education: An Introduction to the Philosophy of Education*. New York: Macmillan, 1916.

———. *The Quest for Certainty: A Study of the Relation of Knowledge and Action*. New York: Minton, Balch & Company, 1929.

Diop, Cheikh Anta. *The African Origin of Civilization: Myth or Reality*. Translated by Mercer Cook. Chicago: Lawrence Hill Books, 1974.

Easterly, William. *The White Man's Burden: Why the West's Efforts to Aid the Rest Have Done So Much Ill and So Little Good*. New York: Penguin Press, 2006.

Ebaugh, Helen Rose, and Janet Saltzman Chafetz. *Religion and the New Immigrants*. Walnut Creek, CA: AltaMira Press, 2000.

Ekeh, Peter P. "Colonialism and the Two Publics in Africa: A Theoretical Statement." *Comparative Studies in Society and History* 17, no. 1 (1975): 91–112.

Einstein, Mara. *Brands of Faith: Marketing Religion in a Commercial Age*. London: Routledge, 2008.

Fanon, Frantz. *The Wretched of the Earth*. Translated by Constance Farrington. New York: Grove Press, 1963.

Feyerabend, Paul. *Against Method: Outline of an Anarchistic Theory of Knowledge*. London: New Left Books, 1975.

Feynman, Richard P. *The Pleasure of Finding Things Out*. New York: Basic Books, 1999.

Freire, Paulo. *Pedagogy of the Oppressed*. New York: Continuum, 1970.

Fromm, Erich. *The Art of Loving*. New York: Harper & Row, 1956.

Geschiere, Peter. *The Modernity of Witchcraft: Politics and the Occult in Postcolonial Africa*. Charlottesville: University Press of Virginia, 1997.

Gifford, Paul. *Christianity, Development and Modernity in Africa*. Oxford: Oxford University Press, 2015.

BIBLIOGRAPHY

Goodin, Robert E. *Protecting the Vulnerable: A Reanalysis of Our Social Responsibilities.* Chicago: University of Chicago Press, 1985.

Habermas, Jürgen. *Between Facts and Norms: Contributions to a Discourse Theory of Law and Democracy.* Cambridge, MA: MIT Press, 1996.

Harari, Yuval Noah. *21 Lessons for the 21st Century.* New York: Spiegel & Grau, 2018.

Harvey, David. *A Brief History of Neoliberalism.* Oxford: Oxford University Press, 2005.

Hayek, Friedrich A. *The Road to Serfdom.* Chicago: University of Chicago Press, 1944.

Hiskett, Mervyn. *The Development of Islam in West Africa.* London: Longman, 1984.

Hoover, Stewart M. *The Media and Religious Authority.* University Park: Pennsylvania State University Press, 2016.

Hume, David. *An Enquiry Concerning Human Understanding.* London: A. Millar, 1748.

James, William. *The Varieties of Religious Experience.* New York: Longmans, Green, and Co., 1902.

Kant, Immanuel. *Groundwork of the Metaphysics of Morals.* Translated by Mary Gregor. Cambridge: Cambridge University Press, 1997.

Kent, Stephen A. *Cults and New Religions: A Brief History.* 2nd ed. Oxford: Oxford University Press, 2016.

Lendman, Stephen, and Januarius J. Asongu. *The Iraq Quagmire: The Price of Imperial Arrogance.* Lawrenceville, GA: Greenview, 2007.

Levitt, Peggy. *God Needs No Passport: Immigrants and the Changing American Religious Landscape.* New York: New Press, 2007.

Locke, John. *Two Treatises of Government.* Cambridge: Cambridge University Press, 1988.

Mbembe, Achille. *On the Postcolony.* Berkeley: University of California Press, 2001.

Mill, John Stuart. *On Liberty.* Indianapolis: Hackett Publishing, 1978.

Nozick, Robert. *Philosophical Explanations.* Cambridge, MA: Belknap Press of Harvard University Press, 1981.

North, Douglass C. *Institutions, Institutional Change, and Economic Performance.* Cambridge: Cambridge University Press, 1990.

Nussbaum, Martha. *Upheavals of Thought: The Intelligence of Emotions.* Cambridge: Cambridge University Press, 2001.

Nyerere, Julius K. *Ujamaa: Essays on Socialism.* Oxford: Oxford University Press, 1968.

Pasquale, Frank. *The Black Box Society: The Secret Algorithms that Control Money and Information.* Cambridge, MA: Harvard University Press, 2015.

Pinker, Steven. *Enlightenment Now: The Case for Reason, Science, Humanism, and Progress.* New York: Viking, 2018.

Popper, Karl R. *Conjectures and Refutations: The Growth of Scientific Knowledge.* London: Routledge, 1963.

BIBLIOGRAPHY

———. *The Logic of Scientific Discovery*. London: Routledge, 1959.

Rawls, John. *A Theory of Justice*. Cambridge, MA: Harvard University Press, 1971.

Richardson, James T. *Regulating Religion: Case Studies from Around the Globe*. New York: Kluwer Academic/Plenum, 2004.

Rieger, Joerg. *Jesus vs. Capitalism?* Minneapolis: Fortress Press, 2018.

Rodney, Walter. *How Europe Underdeveloped Africa*. Washington, DC: Howard University Press, 1972.

Russell, Bertrand. *The Problems of Philosophy*. New York: Henry Holt and Company, 1912.

Sandel, Michael J. *What Money Can't Buy: The Moral Limits of Markets*. New York: Farrar, Straus and Giroux, 2012.

Scanlon, T. M. *What We Owe to Each Other*. Cambridge, MA: Harvard University Press, 1998.

Sen, Amartya. *Development as Freedom*. New York: Alfred A. Knopf, 1999.

Service, Robert. *Comrades! A History of World Communism*. Cambridge, MA: Harvard University Press, 2007.

Shinnie, P. L. *Ancient Nubia*. London: Kegan Paul International, 1996.

Smith, Adam. *The Theory of Moral Sentiments*. Oxford: Oxford University Press, 1976.

Spinoza, Benedict de. *Ethics*. Translated by Edwin Curley. Princeton, NJ: Princeton University Press, 1985.

Stark, Rodney, and Roger Finke. *Acts of Faith: Explaining the Human Side of Religion*. Berkeley: University of California Press, 2000.

Swinburne, Richard. *Miracles*. London: Macmillan, 1989.

Tuchman, Barbara W. *The March of Folly: From Troy to Vietnam*. New York: Knopf, 1984.

United Nations Economic Commission for Africa. *Africa's Development Dynamics 2021*. Addis Ababa: ECA Publications, 2021.

Urban, Hugh B. *The Church of Scientology: A History of a New Religion*. Princeton, NJ: Princeton University Press, 2015.

Walton, Jonathan L. *Watch This! The Ethics and Aesthetics of Black Televangelism*. New York: New York University Press, 2009.

Walzer, Michael. *Spheres of Justice: A Defense of Pluralism and Equality*. New York: Basic Books, 1983.

Weber, Max. *Economy and Society*. Edited by Guenther Roth and Claus Wittich. Berkeley: University of California Press, 1978.

———. *The Protestant Ethic and the Spirit of Capitalism*. Translated by Stephen Kalberg. London: Routledge, 2002.

Wiredu, Kwasi. "Toward Decolonizing African Philosophy and Religion." *African Studies Quarterly* 1, no. 4 (1998): 17–46.

Williams, Bernard. *Truth and Truthfulness: An Essay in Genealogy*. Princeton, NJ: Princeton University Press, 2002.

Zakaria, Fareed. *Ten Lessons for a Post-Pandemic World*. New York: W. W. Norton & Company, 2020.

INDEX

1 Corinthians 13:12, 38, 164
2 Corinthians 5:7, 36
1 Peter 3:15, 36
1 John 1:5, 170

adequation of intellect and reality, 29–30, 36, 53, 101, 165
Acts 17:26-28, 168
agency
   architecture of, 91–93, 117
   epistemic, 24, 38, 94, 115–20, 145–47, 168
AI (artificial intelligence)
   algorithmic absolutism, 49–55
   algorithmic bias, 54, 60
   black box problem, 58–59
   digital realism crisis, 49–55
   epistemology of, 22, 41–68
   ethics of, 57–62, 146
Al-Farabi, 10
analytic philosophy, 18, 25–26
Angels (biblical concept), 39
Anselm of Canterbury, St., 194
architecture
   of agency, 91–93
   of reason, 10, 26
Aristotle, 9–10, 21, 29, 52, 101, 152–53, 166

Asongu, Januarius Jingwa, passim
Augustine of Hippo, St., 29, 80
Auguste Comte, 17–18

Bambui, xl, 194
Benediction: *Prayer of the Rational Heart*, 170
belief
   belief vs. knowledge, 47–50, 76, 90
   psychological function of, 77–78
Boff, Leonardo, 194
Brahman, 15
Buddhism
   Four Noble Truths, 15
   Middle Way, 15–16
Buea (Cameroon), v
Bushu, Immanuel Balanjo (Bishop), v, xl–xli

Cambridge, University of (Wolfson Press Fellowship), 195
Charisma University, 195
civic epistemology, 38–39
coherence criterion, 32, 45, 76, 102
Colossians 2:8, 18
communal personhood, 14–15
Confucianism, 15

INDEX

consciousness
  phenomenological analysis of, 17–18
correspondence criterion, 31, 50, 53, 76, 102
Critical Synthetic Realism (CSR)
  axiological distinction, 35–36
  conceptual model (Appendix I), 177–80
  pillars of, 29–37
  synthetic loop, 29, 44, 89
  and artificial intelligence, 48–55
  and democracy, 137–48
  and development, 85–94
  and education, 189–92
  and prayer, 122–32
critical inquiry, 6–7, 48, 91
critical realism, 21
culture
  epistemic dimensions of, 85–90

Dao (Daoism), 15
Daoism, 15
deepfakes, 52–53
Deuteronomy 30:19, 116
democracy
  epistemic foundations of, 137–39
  critiques of, 141–44
  digital democracy, 146
  planetary democracy, 146–47
determinism, 97–100, 110–11
digital absolutism, 49–55
dogma, epistemic dangers of, 87–89
D'Aquili, Eugene, 127

Ecclesiastes 1:2–11, 167
Ecclesiastes 3:1–8, 117
education
  as liberation, 91–93
  epistemic equity in, 156
Éla, Jean-Marc, 194
empiricism, 12, 31
epistemic addiction, 114

epistemic ecology, 85–86
epistemic fracture, 87–91, 105
epistemic humility, 37–39, 165
epistemic justice, 92, 156
epistemic pluralism, 31–33, 102
epistemic poverty, 89–90
epistemic republic, 145–47, 168
epistemic sovereignty, 115–17
Ephesians 4:25, 35
ethics
  of inquiry, 36
  of freedom, 116
  of prayer, 122–32
  of technology, 146, 156
eudaimonia, 152–59
existentialism, 18
Exodus 3:14, 29

Fanon, Frantz, 194
faith
  faith and reason, 36, 80, 112, 165
fatalism
  ancient roots of, 97–98
  theological forms, 98–99
  psychological dimensions, 107–12
  CSR refutation of, 100–06
falsification, 33–34, 58, 103, 138
fairness
  equality vs. equity, 153
filter bubbles, 51
Fonlon, Bernard Nsokika, v, xxv, xli, 194
Freire, Paulo, 194
freedom
  epistemic foundations of, 24, 37, 105–06, 116–20

Galatians 5:1, 120
Genesis 1:26–28, 87
Genesis 2:7, 49
Genesis 3:1–7, 75
global agency, 24, 38, 94, 119, 168

INDEX

governance
   Integrity Rule in, 92, 119
Greek philosophy, 7–10
Gutiérrez, Gustavo, 194

Häring, Bernard, 194
happiness, 155
healing
   epistemic healing, 38, 82
human flourishing, see *eudaimonia*
Husserl, Edmund, 17–18

ignorance
   as oppression, 26, 90
   illumination (light metaphor), 28, 39, 170
Integrity Rule, 92, 119, 144
Isaiah 1:16–17, 81
Isaiah 55:8–9, 165

James 1:5, 123
James 2:17, 129
Jeremiah 17:9, 111
Jingwa, Nicholas Asongu, xl
Job 38:1–11, 164
John 1:1–5, 49, 97
John 8:32, 24, 63, 146
John 14:6, 29
justice
   epistemic foundations of, 81, 146, 158

Koenig, Harold, 126–27
knowledge
   as moral act, 35–36
   as pilgrimage, 40, 165
   limits of, 164–65

Lekelefac, George Chrysostom Nchumbonga, v, xxiii–xxvi, xli
liberation
   knowledge as liberation, 26, 63, 171

liberation theology, 81, 93
light (metaphor), 28, 39, 170
logos, 49, 97
Luke 12:48, 116

Marcel, Gabriel, 126–27
machine learning, 43–48
Mark 4:24–25, 65
Matthew 6:10, 130
Matthew 7:7–11, 123, 127
Matthew 25:14–30, 129
Mbiti, John, 15
meaning
   mortality and, 167
metaphysical realism, 29–31, 101
Micah 6:8, 146
miracles, epistemic critique of, 128

Newberg, Andrew, 126–27
neuropsychology
   of freedom, 111
Newman, John Henry, 194
Ngangsic-Asongu, Bernard
Nkengbeza, xxxix
Ngangsic-Asongu, Christine, xxxix–xl
Ngangsic-Asongu, Jude Jingwa, xxxix
Ngangsic-Asongu, Maria Yorkza, xxxix
Nkengbeza, Monique, xl

occult causality, 74–76, 90
ontology, 7–8, 49
oppression
   epistemic roots of, 26, 90

phenomenology, 17–18
pilgrimage (knowledge as), 40, 165
Pontifical Urban University (Rome), 194
political philosophy, 137–48
positivism, 17–18
postmodernism, 18–19

INDEX

power
    knowledge and, 59
prayer
    ethical critique of, 122–32
Proverbs 1:7, 36
Proverbs 4:7, 152
Proverbs 14:12, 105
providence
    general vs. partial, 130–31
Psalms 8:4–6, 152
Psalms 19:1–4, 166
Psalms 119:105, 170

Rahner, Karl, 194
reason
    moral responsibility of, 26, 65, 146
relativism, rejection of, 18–19, 31
religion
    distortion of faith, 80
Romans 1:20, 166
Romans 8:28, 130
Romans 12:2, 91

science
    limits of, 34, 166
self-correction, 34, 139
Saint Monica University, xxvi, xxxii, xli, 194
social epistemology, 34
St. Thomas Aquinas Major Seminary (STAMS), v, xl, 194

superstition, 73–82, 90
sustainability, 154, 157

Tanla-Kishani, Andrew Bongasu, v, xxv, xl–xli, 194
technology
    ethical limits of, 39, 146, 169
testimony
    collapse of, 144
therapy
    philosophy as therapy, 82, 114
truth
    correspondence theory of, 29–31
    ethical obligation of, 35–36
    aesthetic dimension of, 39
    truth as liberation, 63, 171
Tutu, Desmond, 15

Ubuntu, 14–15
utility
    rejection as truth criterion, 35

Veritatis Splendor (John Paul II), xxviii
virtue
    intellectual virtue, 36, 81

wisdom
    moral apex of knowledge, 67
Wiredu, Kwasi, 15
witchcraft
    philosophical refutation of, 73–82